PUBLIC FINANCING OF
CONGRESSIONAL ELECTIONS

PUBLIC FINANCING OF CONGRESSIONAL ELECTIONS

R. SAM GARRETT

Novinka Books
New York

NOTICE TO THE READER

LIBRARY OF CONGRESS CATALOGING-IN-PUBLICATION DATA
Garrett,R. Sam.
 Public financing of congressional elections / R. Sam Garrett.
        p. cm.
ISBN 978-1-60456-684-0(softcover)
      1.   Campaign funds—United States. 2. United States. Congress—Elections. I. Title.
      JK1991.G34   2008
      324.7'8—dc22   20080018968

Published by Nova Science Publishers, Inc. ✦ *New York*

CONTENTS

Preface   vii

Introduction   1

**Legislative Proposals for Public
Financing of Congressional Elections**   11

State Experiences with Public Financing   43

**Public Opinion on Public Financing and
Spending Limits**   63

**Potential Considerations for Congressional
Public Financing**   65

**Appendix 1. Public Finance Bills Passed
by the House or Senate: 1973 – 1993**   69

**Appendix 2. Public Finance Bills in the
109th Congress: Summary of Key Provisions**   79

**Appendix 3. Public Finance Bills in the
110th Congress: Summary of Key Provisions**   87

References   97

Index   113

PREFACE

Since the early 20th century, Congress has considered legislation regarding campaign finance in federal elections and has enacted major statutes to prevent real or apparent corruption and to curb undue influence by wealthy individuals and interest groups. That legislation has required disclosure, limited or banned certain funding sources, or limited certain expenditures.

To critics, public campaign financing, generally in conjunction with spending limits, is the ultimate solution to perceived problems arising from ever-growing costs of campaigns and the accompanying need for privately donated campaign funds. Public financing supporters maintain that replacing private funds with public money would most effectively reduce potentially corrupting influence from "interested" money. On the other hand, opponents of public financing question whether real or apparent corruption from private fundraising is as serious a problem as critics claim. They also argue that public financing would be an inappropriate use of taxpayer dollars and would compel taxpayers to fund candidates they find objectionable.

In the early 1970s, supporters succeeded in enacting public financing in presidential elections, a system which has been available since 1976. In addition, many states and localities have provided public financing in their elections since the 1970s (or before). Today, 16 states offer some form of direct aid to candidates' campaigns through fixed subsidies or matching funds. Perceptions about the presidential and state public financing systems have shaped opinions about adding public financing to congressional elections. Also shaping that debate was the Supreme Court's landmark 1976 *Buckley v. Valeo* ruling, which struck down mandatory spending limits, but sanctioned voluntary spending limits accompanying public financing.

Proposals for publicly funded congressional elections have been offered in almost every Congress since 1956; the issue was prominently debated in the mid-1970s and the late 1980s through early 1990s. Proposals were passed twice by the Senate in the 93rd Congress and by both the House and Senate in the 101st, 102nd, and 103rd Congresses. Only the 102nd Congress proposal was reconciled in conference but was vetoed by the President. In the 101st through 103rd Congresses, resistance to public funding was sufficiently strong, in part reflecting perceived lack of public support, that the role of public funds per se was reduced, while the broader concept of public benefits (more indirect or government-mandated assistance to candidates) became more prominent in Congress. Four 110th Congress bills (H.R. 1614, H.R. 2817, S. 936, and S. 1285) would extend public financing to congressional elections.

This book reviews past proposals for and debate over congressional public financing. It also discusses experiences with the presidential and state public financing systems. Finally, the report offers potential considerations for Congress in devising a public financing system for its elections if it chooses to do so.

INTRODUCTION[1]

OVERVIEW OF REPORT

This first section provides the context for the debate on extending public financing to congressional elections, beginning with a discussion of two major political realities that inform that debate. The first is the presidential public financing system that has been in place since 1976 and has had mixed success in realizing the goals of its original sponsors. The second is the interplay between the concepts of public financing and campaign spending limits, which are often linked but which have very distinct characteristics; the 1976 landmark Supreme Court decision in *Buckley v. Valeo* contributed to that linkage because of its allowance for only *voluntary* spending limits, such as in conjunction with a public financing system. The section concludes with a summary of arguments for and against public financing, arguments which have not changed in essence over time but which have been shaped by the political realities noted above.

The second section provides a historical review of efforts in Congress to enact public financing of its elections (although some attention is paid to presidential public financing as a precursor). The section begins with a brief review of early congressional interest and activity in the 20th century, followed by a more detailed Congress-by-Congress discussion beginning with the 90th Congress. Special attention is paid to the two periods in which congressional activity on public financing was the greatest: the Watergate-focused 93rd Congress and the 100th —103rd Congresses. Public finance bills were passed by at least one chamber in those two periods, although the latter period was marked by a move toward downplaying public funds per se in favor of the broader concept of public benefits. The section concludes with a review of the major features of congressional proposals, presented as policy options to choose from in devising a congressional public finance system.

The third section examines the experience of the 16 states which provide some form of public subsidies to candidates for state office. This section features a table (Table 1) detailing these systems, and concludes with an analysis of the impact of public finance programs in the states.

The fourth section offers a discussion of public opinion data on support for public financing of elections, as well as for the related idea of campaign spending limits. Public opinion is not as extensive on these questions as in the 1970s, when the idea of public financing was particularly prominent.

The final section reviews the experience from public finance systems at both the state and presidential levels to offer some overarching observations for Congress possibly to consider in devising a public finance system for its elections, should it choose to do so.

The report concludes with three appendices, to augment the information in the section on congressional proposals. The first appendix is a table (Table 2) providing details of the public finance (or benefits) measures that have passed either chamber (from 1973 - 1993); because they passed at least one chamber, these bills are perhaps the most important for Congress to review before beginning a fresher look at the idea. To allow a more contemporary look at how recent public finance proposals have evolved, the second appendix provides a summary of the four public finance bills proposed in the 109th Congress. A third appendix provides a summary of public financing bills introduced (as of this writing) in the 110th Congress.

UNDERPINNINGS OF CONTEMPORARY CONGRESSIONAL DEBATE

While public financing of congressional elections has been advocated for a century, contemporary discussions of these proposals are informed by two basic political realities of the past 30 years. First, the nation has had public financing in presidential elections since 1976, and that system serves both as a model for proposals to extend it to congressional elections and as a case study of how a congressional system should and should not be structured. Second, in striking down mandatory expenditure limits in 1976 while allowing voluntary limits in the context of a public finance system, the Supreme Court's *Buckley v. Valeo*[2] ruling resulted in a closer linkage in the minds of policymakers between the distinct concepts of public subsidies for election campaigns and limitations on campaign spending.

Presidential System Since the 1970s: A Model

Since 1976, public funds have helped finance presidential elections, with the level of funds determined by a taxpayer designations on a voluntary checkoff. This system was established initially under the Revenue Act of 1971[3] and augmented by the Federal Election Campaign Act (FECA) Amendments of 1974.[4] Candidates who meet eligibility requirements and agree to voluntary limits on campaign expenditures are eligible for matching funds in the primaries. In the general election, major party candidates automatically qualify for full subsidies equal to the spending limit (in 2004, John Kerry and George W. Bush each received $74.6 million for their fall campaigns); minor party and independent candidates may also qualify for public funds by meeting specified criteria. Also, political parties may receive funding for their nominating conventions. As of June 2006, $1.435 billion has been "checked off" since the option first appeared on tax forms in 1973, and candidates and parties have received $1.332 billion in this manner since the 1976 election.

After three decades, presidential election public funding is by no means a universally supported program, as reflected in declining taxpayer checkoffs (from a high of 28.7% of taxpayers checking "yes" on 1980 returns to 9.2% doing so on 2004 returns), attempts in the 102nd and 104th Congresses to end the system, and decisions by major candidates to forgo public funding in the 2000 and 2004 primaries. While supporters say that the system has curbed campaign spending and reliance on private resources, opponents point to the large amounts of private funds spent in unregulated ways, thus undermining the spending limits — a prime reason for giving public funds.

Underlying most evaluations are sharply opposing views of public funding, a divergence little changed from the start. Supporters see it as a democratic, egalitarian system, offering the best chance to reduce the potentially corrosive effects of money on the political process and renew public confidence in that process. Opponents see public funding as a waste of tax money, which artificially skews the results and forces taxpayers to fund candidates whom they oppose.

While candidate-controlled spending (subject to limits) may have been curbed from pre-1976 levels, other forms of spending to benefit candidates have emerged which have increasingly served to circumvent the spending limits. Even in the general election, in which major party nominees are "fully funded" with public monies, additional spending by parties and groups has arguably undermined the intent of overall limits (most notably through party soft money,[5] issue advocacy messages, and activities by groups operating under Section 527 of the Internal Revenue Code[6]). Critics view this as an inherent obstacle to efforts to limit spending; supporters see it as a problem that can and should be corrected to protect the integrity of the system.

Few would argue that the presidential public finance system has freed candidates from dependence on private money, but to the extent that large amounts of public funds have been available, money's perceived influence may have declined. Moreover, what many see as the burden and distraction of fundraising has been lessened, particularly for major party nominees. It is also true, however, that soft money has allowed the wealthy again to make very large donations, through the parties up until 2002 and most recently through 527 organizations, raising issues comparable to those raised by the system in place prior to FECA.

Public funding supporters argue that the system has helped unknown candidates attain far greater visibility, even to reach the point of nomination and election. In three of the eight presidential elections from 1976 to 2004 in which an incumbent was seeking reelection, a challenger (historically underfunded) has defeated an incumbent President.

While it is undeniable that the system forces taxpayers in effect to fund candidates they may find repugnant, the prediction that public funding would encourage fringe candidacies and thus "waste" public resources has largely not been realized. Counting Lyndon LaRouche (who ran as a Democrat from 1980 to 2004) and 11 minor party candidates who qualified for funding as "fringe" candidates, and adding the $12.6 million in subsidies paid to the Reform Party for its 2000 convention, CRS calculations based on data compiled by the Federal Election Commission (FEC) show that the $64.2 million they received is only 4.8% of all public funding since 1976.[7]

The relative support and acceptance of public funding has varied. Support has been strong among candidates (at least until 2000), the media, citizens' groups, and various outside panels studying the political process. But mass public acceptance has not developed. Low checkoff rates mirror the fairly consistent opposition in opinion polls to public financing per se, although support generally rises when the question is posed as public funding *with* limits on spending and interest groups. (Public opinion about public financing and expenditure limits is discussed later in this report.)

Opponents note that public financing has not stemmed the decline in confidence in the political system registered in opinion polls of the past 30 years. Supporters say that such data argue for further reforms in the system and even the extension of public funding to congressional races. They also insist that one must consider how much worse the presidential system might be today were it not for public funding (especially given the limits on contributions without mandatory spending limits). Critics do not disagree that presidential elections are cleaner today than before 1976, but insist that FECA's disclosure provisions and funding source limits are far more important factors than public funding. Even among those who generally support the presidential public funding system, concerns that structural problems have greatly eroded the system's value have led to recent calls for major amendments to bolster it. Thus, while the presidential public funding system is an integral part of elections today, its future is by no means certain.[8]

Linkage with Spending Limits

At the outset of any discussion on public financing proposals, it is important to address the question of expenditure limits because, almost invariably, legislative proposals for public funding are linked with candidates' adherence to spending limits. Despite this common linkage, public financing and spending limits are distinct concepts, with distinct potential benefits and drawbacks. Public financing of elections, at its core, is aimed at reducing reliance by politicians on private, interested sources of money for their elections. Expenditure limits are essentially aimed at curbing rising and, in the view of many, excessive amounts of money spent on elections.

In fact, from the time public financing was first proposed by President Theodore Roosevelt in 1907 until the Supreme Court's 1976 ruling in *Buckley v. Valeo* (424 U.S. 1 (1976)), the impetus for passage stemmed more from the concern over the source of campaign money than the overall amount spent. In that landmark ruling, the Court struck down mandatory spending limits (such as those imposed on congressional candidates by the FECA Amendments of 1974), but allowed that in a *voluntary* system of public financing, it was permissible to require candidate adherence to spending limits as a condition of a government-provided benefit (i.e., public funds).[9] Hence, spending limits in conjunction with public funding would be permissible because candidates voluntarily accepted them.

In light of the *Buckley* decision, the prevailing view among policymakers has been that public financing offers the only realistic means of controlling campaign expenditures in congressional elections, short of enacting a constitutional amendment to allow mandatory limits (which Congress has refused to support on several occasions). Furthermore, the impetus for such a plan has appeared to shift more toward controlling the level of spending than toward addressing the source of campaign money, although the two are closely related. Indeed, even some who have had reservations about public financing have moved to support it, as a last resort, to curb rising campaign costs.

Invariably, assessments of potential effects of public funding are often tangled up with those of the expenditure limits which generally accompany them. While there are distinct reasons to favor public funding per se, perhaps its greatest appeal has become its inducement to candidate acceptance of spending limits. It is important to distinguish between the comparative merits and potential drawbacks of each, however. Opponents of proposals advanced in recent years have charged that public financing would constitute an "incumbent protection" measure. Yet, that charge appears more appropriately leveled against spending limits, not public funding. It is widely believed among political scientists that spending limits, equally applied to both candidates in a race, would tend to work to the advantage of the incumbent, who begins with greater name recognition and the resources associated with office.[10] While the spending limit aspect of a public finance system may thus help incumbents more than challengers, it is also arguable that public subsidies (and cost-reducing public benefits) could assist the challenger more than the incumbent, especially where the challenger is, as is often the case, greatly under funded compared with the incumbent.

But if the political science community has generally looked with greater favor on public funding (to enhance competition) than on spending limits (which could stifle competition),[11] it is also the case that public opinion has generally taken an opposite view. As is discussed later in this report, opinion surveys invariably register strong public support for the belief that too much money is spent on elections today and for spending limits as a solution. Findings of support for public financing per se, however, are mixed, at best. This appears to reflect differences in how questions are worded, but there does appear to be a strong resistance to the concept of using taxpayer money on elections.[12]

The dichotomy between the perspectives of election scholars and the general public helps to explain the course of the debate on public finance proposals over the past 30 years. The greater public support for spending limits than public financing explains why, during the intensive debate in the 101st through the 103rd Congresses (discussed below), the major challenge of spending-limit supporters was to reduce the role of public funds in their proposals. As bills advanced in those Congresses, the goal invariably became to minimize the role of public funds, even if only to make it more indirect.

Thus, the perceptions of public opinion can help explain the progress or lack thereof of public financing proposals in recent years.

It should be noted that some of the goals sought in the public funding and spending limit measures have been addressed in other legislation, less sweeping yet often with significant bipartisan support. Proposals to lower campaign costs, without spending limits, have been prominent in Congress at least until enactment of the Bipartisan Campaign Reform Act of 2002 (BCRA). Bills to provide free or reduced-rate broadcast time and postal rates have sought to reduce campaign costs and the need for money, without the possibly negative effects of arbitrary limits. Bills to provide for tax credits for small individual contributions have sought to encourage a greater role for citizens vis-a-vis organized interest groups. These measures offer the potential of realizing some of the aims of the more comprehensive measures but without some of the perceived pitfalls.

ARGUMENTS SUPPORTING AND OPPOSING PUBLIC FINANCING: BRIEF OVERVIEW

Supporting

A few major points are common arguments in favor of public financing. Supporters say that public financing can reduce the threat of political corruption, enhance electoral competition, and allow candidates to focus on issues rather than raising money. To many observers, the amount of money spent in elections today is arguably corrupting the political system, forcing candidates and officeholders to spend increasing amounts of time raising money, possibly creating pressure on them to rely on affluent individuals and special interests for campaign assistance, conceivably deterring candidates without personal fortunes from attempting to run for office, and leaving an impression among some voters that elections are "bought and sold." Accordingly, one of the most prominent goals behind public financing is reducing the potential for corruption or the appearance of corruption. As political scientists Donald A. Gross and Robert K. Goidel have explained, "Public subsidies to candidates, whether in the form of direct grants or matching funds, are seen as a way to minimize the undue influence and corruption often ascribed to contributors and partisan fundraising."[13] Many former lawmakers, interest group representatives, political professionals, and academic experts submitted written testimony for the *McConnell v. FEC* lawsuit heard by a U.S. District Court and the Supreme

Court of the United States in their consideration of BCRA. Some of this testimony included empirical analysis of claims about potentially corrupting influences from private money in campaign politics and related issues.[14]

Other public financing goals relate to electoral competition. Public financing provides candidates — regardless of personal wealth — with financial resources to wage campaigns.[15] This allows candidates who might not otherwise run for office to do so. As is noted in the discussion of states' experiences with public financing, most programs require that candidates demonstrate political viability before being eligible for funds. If more candidates have access to funds, supporters say that electoral competition should increase.

Finally, public financing is attractive to some because it is one of the few constitutional ways to limit campaign spending — a major concern among campaign reformers. Although the Supreme Court's 1976 *Buckley v. Valeo* ruling held that campaign spending generally could not be subjected to mandatory limits, candidates *could* be required to limit spending in exchange for receiving public funding. As is discussed elsewhere in this report, some public financing systems — including the presidential one — are today in jeopardy because major candidates fear that observing spending limits associated with public financing will preclude them from spending enough money to wage competitive campaigns.

Opposing

Objections to public financing are also varied. Many are rooted in philosophical opposition to funding elections with taxpayer money, compelling taxpayers to support candidates whose views are antithetical to theirs, and adding another government program in the face of some cynicism toward government spending. Opponents also raise administrative concerns: how can a system be devised that accounts for different natures of districts and states, with different styles of campaigning and disparate media costs, and is fair to all candidates — incumbent, challenger, or open-seat, major or minor party, serious or "longshot"? Similarly, opponents assert that public financing could distort elections by imposing the same system on 50 different states with different degrees of competitiveness in individual races and by providing even greater advantages to incumbents than already exist, thereby decreasing the competitiveness of elections. In view of the relatively low rate of participation in the voluntary checkoff for the existing presidential system (9.2% of taxpayers checked "yes" on their 2004 tax returns when asked if they wanted to fund the system), they see little evidence that the public would favor such a plan.

Some public financing opponents believe that government-funded campaign subsides amount to "welfare for politicians,"[16] and are an inappropriate use of taxpayer dollars.[17] These opponents argue that public financing could coerce candidates into limiting their campaign spending — viewed as a form of political speech — in exchange for funding, or that it could force taxpayers to indirectly fund campaign messages they might find objectionable. On a related note, opponents suggest that public financing could waste taxpayer money on "fringe" candidates who represent political views that may be far outside the mainstream and who have little chance of winning elections.[18]

In response to arguments that public funding is necessary to limit campaign expenditures, those opposed to public financing often argue that campaign spending is not high, especially compared with commercial advertising budgets or spending on consumer goods.[19] They argue that worthy candidates will win public support without government intervention via public financing. Some researchers also suggest that concerns about rising campaign costs are overstated, and that most campaign fundraising comes from individuals who give less than the legal limit.[20]

Finally, opponents of public financing sometimes argue that proponents fail to sufficiently support their arguments in favor of public financing, relying instead on the "self-evidence" of its appeal.[21] For example, although the appearance of corruption or potential corruption is a common argument in favor of public financing, political scientists Jeffrey Milyo and David Primo have found that scholarly research on the topic is limited or anecdotal. The same, they say, is true for fears about declining trust in government and declining voter turnout, which some contend could be buoyed by public financing.[22]

LEGISLATIVE PROPOSALS FOR PUBLIC FINANCING OF CONGRESSIONAL ELECTIONS

While the idea of public financing of federal elections was first proposed in 1907, it was not until the 1950s that bills were first introduced in Congress to implement such a plan. Since that time, legislative proposals have been offered in nearly every Congress, while the extent of legislative activity around the issue has varied according to the political climate and circumstances. In two very active periods, bills to extend public financing to congressional elections have passed one or both houses but were never enacted.

In the first period, during the 93rd Congress (1973-1974), the Senate twice passed bills for public funding in congressional elections, widely seen as a response to the unfolding Watergate scandal.[23] In 1973, a bill was passed providing full subsidies (equal to mandatory spending limits) to major party candidates in House and Senate general elections. In 1974, a bill was passed providing matching funds in House and Senate primaries and full subsidies (equal to the voluntary spending limits) to major party candidates in House and Senate general elections. Both provisions were later deleted in conference, in view of some strong opposition in the House.

In the second period, the 100th through 103rd Congresses (1987-1993), the House and Senate spent considerable amounts of time debating bills that featured the twin ideas of voluntary spending limits and public financing. In the 101st, 102nd, and 103rd Congresses, both chambers actually passed such bills; the 102nd Congress bill was vetoed by President George H.W. Bush, but the bills in the other two Congresses were never reconciled in conference.

In contrast to the first period, when one of the Senate-passed bills covered both primary and general elections, bills in the second period offered benefits only for general election candidates. More broadly, efforts in the more recent period reflected a move toward paring down the level of public treasury funds going to campaigns, in light of a less favorable political climate. The emphasis in this second period shifted from public *funds* per se to public *benefits*. Public benefits were those either financed with public resources — whether directly, as with public subsidies, or indirectly, as with revenue forgone from tax incentives or postal discounts — or mandated by government action, such as requirements for reduced broadcast rates, at no cost to the U.S. Treasury. The common element was that they all constituted incentives to participation in a voluntary system based on campaign spending limits.

Evolution During the Early 20th Century

The earliest suggestion to Congress of public subsidies for election campaigns was apparently made by President Theodore Roosevelt in 1907 in his annual message to Congress. Roosevelt saw reforms such as requiring disclosure and prohibiting corporate contributions as worthwhile but difficult to enforce and inadequate in deterring "an unscrupulous man of unlimited means from buying his own way into office." He suggested an admittedly radical approach of providing ample appropriations to the major national political parties to fund their "organization and machinery." Parties receiving federal monies were to be limited to a fixed amount that could be raised from individual contributors, all of which would be disclosed to the public. It is unclear from the text of his message (the relevant portion of which is reprinted below) whether Roosevelt intended this plan to be limited to presidential, as opposed to all federal, campaigns. At the time, given the political parties' central role in financing all election campaigns, the distinction may not have been as great as it would be today, when candidates take the lead role in financing their campaigns. In any case, the section of the message was titled "Presidential Campaign Expenses."

> Under our form of government voting is not merely a right but a duty, and, moreover, a fundamental and necessary duty if a man is to be a good citizen. It is well to provide that corporations shall not contribute to Presidential or National campaigns, and furthermore to provide for the

publication of both contributions and expenditures. There is, however, always danger in laws of this kind, which from their very nature are difficult of enforcement; the danger being lest they be obeyed only by the honest, and disobeyed by the unscrupulous, so as to act only as a penalty upon honest men. Moreover, no such law would hamper an unscrupulous man of unlimited means from buying his own way into office. There is a very radical measure which would, I believe, work a substantial improvement in our system of conducting a campaign, although I am well aware that it will take some time for people so to familiarize themselves with such a proposal as to be willing to consider its adoption. The need for collecting large campaign funds would vanish if Congress provided an appropriation for the proper and legitimate expenses of each of the great national parties, an appropriation ample enough to meet the necessity for thorough organization and machinery, which requires a large expenditure of money. Then the stipulation should be made that no party receiving campaign funds from the Treasury should accept more than a fixed amount from any individual subscriber or donor; and the necessary publicity for receipts and expenditures could without difficulty be provided.[24]

Roosevelt was not exaggerating when he commented that it would take "some time" for people to familiarize themselves with such a proposal.

From the mid-1920s through the 1970s, select and special committees had been established by every Congress (predominantly on the Senate side) to investigate campaign expenditures — presidential or congressional — in recent elections. Reports issued at the conclusion of the work of these committees often included recommendations designed to correct shortcomings perceived in existing campaign finance practices. In 1937, during the 75th Congress, the report of the Senate's Special Committee to Investigate Campaign Expenditures of Presidential, Vice Presidential, and Senatorial Candidates in 1936 was released. Included in its section of recommendations was a proposal for public funding of all federal elections, which the committee passed along without judgment as to its merits. All private contributions were to be prohibited under this plan. Under recommendation no. 9, the report said,

It has been suggested that private contributions to political campaigns be prohibited entirely and that instead all election campaign expenses should be defrayed from public funds.[25]

Congress apparently took no action on this proposal.

Interest in public funding of political campaigns has often been aroused by allegations of unethical conduct by public officials for accepting particular campaign contributions. Such was the case on July 6, 1949, when Senator Henry Cabot Lodge, Jr., introduced a resolution to commission a study by the Committee on Rules and Administration on the mechanics of establishing a system of public funding of presidential campaigns. In introducing his resolution, Lodge responded to rumors government corruption.[26] The resolution — S.Res. 132 — read as follows:

> Resolved. That the Senate Committee on Rules and Administration is authorized and directed to make a full and complete study and investigation for the purpose of obtaining such information with respect to the problems involved in financing with governmental funds presidential election campaigns in the United States as may be necessary to enable the committee to formulate and report at the earliest practicable date a bill providing for such method of financing presidential election campaigns. [27]

Lodge's support for this concept, the details of which he envisioned coming out of a congressional study, was summed up in this excerpt from his floor statement:

> All this talk of an "office market," and of putting high executive and diplomatic positions on the auction block — all this breeding of suspicion and cynicism would disappear, I believe, overnight if the primary cause of the evil were obliterated at its root. If no private individual or officer of a corporation were permitted by statute to contribute one cent to a presidential campaign there would be a far cleaner atmosphere surrounding political appointments, and this would encourage public-spirited men holding public office. If there are no bidders, there can be no auction.[28]

Lodge acknowledged that the same principle could also be applied to other offices, but he was limiting his suggestion to presidential races because of the enormous number of appointments to public office at the President's disposal. Apparently the type of corruption which motivated Lodge in S.Res. 132 was the selling of government positions rather than the broader notion of trading influence or access on policy questions for campaign contributions. A concern over the latter possibility would be a likely prerequisite for any proposal for public financing of congressional campaigns. No action was taken on S.Res. 132 by the Committee on Rules and Administration.

First Public Finance Bills

During the 84th Congress, the name of Theodore Roosevelt was invoked when the first public funding bills were introduced in Congress, almost 50 years after being suggested by Roosevelt. On February 20, 1956, Senator Richard Neuberger introduced S. 3242, to provide for direct public subsidies for all major party campaigns for federal office, co-sponsored initially by Senators Wayne Morse, James Murray, Paul Douglas, John Sparkman, and Mike Mansfield. The identical bill was submitted two days later in the House as H.R. 9488 by Representative Frank Thompson. "Sometimes I call my bill the Teddy Roosevelt bill, because of its origin," observed Neuberger;[29] Thompson commented that the bill could "appropriately, enough, I think be called the Theodore Roosevelt Campaign Contributions Act of 1956."[30]

Neuberger, who quickly became identified as the chief congressional proponent of public financing at the time,[31] declared that S. 3242 was "the most far-reaching bill ever proposed to strike loose the financial fetters from our democratic processes of government."[32] The final impetus for the bill was the recent revelation of a large campaign contribution offered to a Senator by an oil company during debate on removing federal controls from natural gas prices. The alleged bribery attempt contributed to Neuberger's view that,

> These contributions, in my opinion, have become an unbearable yoke to many of the men who must accept them. They even have become onerous and objectionable to the individuals who parcel out such contributions.[33]

Neuberger based his proposal on the belief that the system of raising campaign funds from private sources hampered the independence of public officials, created doubts among the public about the integrity of the government, and created an inequality in gaining access to voters by various candidates. He continued in his statement to articulate what would remain the major motivation for later advocates of publicly financed elections:

> An undemocratic element is introduced when one nominee can eclipse his opponent not because of superiority of ability or of his policies, but merely through a preponderance of coin of the realm[34]....We would not dream of permitting our Presidents or our Senators and Representatives to draw their pay from a private payroll or in the form of private contributions; they get paid by the public for whom they act. Why, then, leave their campaigns for these offices to be lavishly financed from private sources?[35]

Neuberger's bill provided for the allotment of federal funds to the major political parties, to be used for campaign expenditures of its candidates for federal office. (In the 1950s, election financing was still substantially conducted by the parties, in contrast with today, when party support is considered ancillary to the expenditures of the candidates themselves.) A major party was defined as one which received at least 10% of the vote in the previous national election. The total federal contribution for a two-year period would be determined by multiplying 20 cents by the average number of votes cast in the previous two presidential elections (for presidential election years) and 15 cents by the average number of votes cast in the previous two House elections (for non-presidential election years). The system would be conducted on a voluntary basis and would allow for parties to accept donations from private sources, provided that no individual's contribution exceeded $100 and that the total raised from these sources did not exceed the total federal donation. The term "matching funds" was used by Neuberger to describe the system, but it differed from the present system of matching funds in presidential primaries in that the federal subsidy in the latter case is determined by the amount raised privately; in the Neuberger proposal, the amount that could be raised privately was to be determined by how much the federal subsidy would be. The proposed system was to be administered by a Federal Campaign Contributions Board, to include an administrator and one representative from each major party.

1950s and 1960s

During the 1950s and 1960s, Congress turned its attention to the Federal Corrupt Practices Act,[36] the law governing campaign financing since 1925, and to its perceived inadequacies both in limiting amounts of money raised and spent in elections and in promoting transparency. Numerous hearings were held and bills introduced aimed at improving the nation's campaign finance laws generally. A few bills providing direct public financing were introduced in nearly every Congress since the 84th Congress (1955-1956), but most of these were proposed and supported by a small minority of Members. A greater number of proposals, in this period, however, did include indirect public financing of elections, in the form of tax credits and deductions.

In 1962, a report was released by the President's Commission on Campaign Costs, established the previous year by President John F. Kennedy to make recommendations for improving campaign finance practices and laws.[37] While the report was ostensibly focused on presidential elections, its findings were more broadly applicable to all federal elections because of the extent to which the political parties were at that time the major financiers of all federal campaigns. Its recommendations, which included tax incentives to encourage individual donations to political parties, did not include the proposal urged on it by many for direct public subsidies. Rather, the commission expressed concern for public financing's potential to discourage citizen participation in campaigns, to redistribute power arbitrarily within the parties, to encourage fraud, and to be administered unfairly. However, the commission expressed interest in a "matching incentive system," whereby small individual donations to parties would be equally matched with U.S. Treasury funds. Such a system found favor with the commission because the amount of subsidy would be determined not by governmental action but by "private voluntary action."[38] The 1962 commission report thus advanced the concept of direct government subsidies of campaigns for federal office.

In 1966, Congress took its first step toward public subsidies in federal elections when it enacted the Presidential Campaign Fund Act, providing public subsidies to major political parties for their presidential campaigns. The proposal, sponsored by Senator Russell Long (and which he initially introduced as S. 3469), was added by the Senate Finance Committee as an amendment to H.R. 13103, the Foreign Investors Tax Act. The act was signed into law November 13, 1966, by President Johnson, as P.L. 89-809. The following year, amidst congressional pressure to repeal the act, an amendment was added to the Investment Tax Credit bill (H.R. 6950) to make the act inoperative until Congress provided written guidelines on how the funds were to be distributed. With approval of the bill as P.L. 90-26, the Presidential Campaign Fund Act was effectively killed before it was ever implemented.

CONGRESSIONAL ACTIVITY SINCE THE MID-1960S

90th Congress (1967-1968)

In the 90th Congress, the first public finance bill that covered congressional elections was reported from committee. As reported by the Senate Finance Committee,[39] H.R. 4890, the Honest Elections Act of 1967, provided for optional public financing for general election campaigns of presidential, vice presidential, and senatorial candidates (the committee left the extension of the system to House elections to that body). The system was based on permanent appropriations of the funding necessary, with the stipulation that no private funds could be raised from 60 days before to 30 days after the general election. Funds were to be provided directly to candidates, not through the parties, as earlier bills had done, perhaps in recognition of the onset of candidacies in the 1960s that were more independent of the party structure. The bill was opposed by the committee's six Republican members, who protested its financial burden to taxpayers and its unfairness to taxpayers who were thus forced to support candidates they opposed. The measure never came to the Senate for a vote.

92nd Congress (1971-1972)

The 92nd Congress marked a milestone in the federal government's evolving role in election finance, with enactment of FECA to replace the Corrupt Practices Act of 1925 as the nation's chief statute governing campaign finance and also the enactment of public financing in presidential general elections. The latter was added as a floor amendment by Senator John Pastore during Senate consideration of the Revenue Act of 1971. It set up the Presidential Election Campaign Fund, financed through a $1 tax checkoff (as was first enacted in 1966), to fund presidential general election campaigns. The Pastore amendment also included tax credits and deductions for political contributions, an indirect form of public financing. The amendment survived Senate debate and the House-Senate conference; the underlying legislation survived a veto threat by President Nixon by delaying implementation of the public finance system to the 1976 election. The Revenue Act of 1971 was signed into law December 10, 1971 (P.L. 92-178).

93rd Congress (1973-1974)

In the 93rd Congress, public financing of elections became a major and continuing issue before Congress for the first time, largely in response to the Watergate scandal unfolding in 1973 and 1974. To the extent that large and unaccountable sums of campaign money seemed to be connected to the scandal, many Members came to see the newly enacted FECA of 1971, which essentially required uniform disclosure of campaign money, as inadequate in preventing the kinds of abuses then being uncovered. In addition, public financing of presidential elections was not due to begin until 1976. Those focusing on campaign finance law amendments came to center on the ideas of limits on contributions and expenditures, and on extending public financing to congressional elections. Some 76 bills were introduced in the House and Senate to provide direct subsidies in congressional elections; in the House, more than 140 Members cosponsored such bills.

In July 1973, public finance supporters, led by Senators Edward Kennedy and Hugh Scott, tried to add congressional public funding to the 1973 FECA Amendments. The Kennedy-Scott amendment (no. 406) to S. 372 would have provided public subsidies in House and Senate general elections, with major party candidates eligible for a subsidy equal to the proposed spending limit. The amendment was tabled on a 53-38 vote.[40]

Later in 1973, the Senate passed public financing of congressional elections, the first time either chamber had ever done so. It took the form of amendment no. 651, offered by Senators Kennedy, Scott, and others, to H.R. 11104, the Public Debt Ceiling bill. As added on the Senate floor by a 52-40 vote, the amendment provided for mandatory public financing in House and Senate general elections.[41] Major party House candidates were eligible to receive the greater of 15 cents per eligible voter, or $90,000; major party Senate candidates were eligible for the greater of 15 cents per eligible voter, or $175,000; private contributions were essentially eliminated in the general election (minor party candidates were eligible for funding based on their parties' vote share in the previous election). H.R. 11104, as amended, passed the Senate that day by a 58-34 vote.[42] This provision was removed, however, when the House refused to accept the Senate amendments.[43] A leadership agreement resulted in the matter being dropped from the public debt limit bill and killing the issue for the first session of the 93rd Congress.[44] (See Appendix 1 for details on this measure.)

By 1974, after a year of the unfolding Watergate scandal, support for public financing of elections was growing in Congress. In February 1974, the Senate Rules and Administration Committee reported a new version of the FECA Amendments (in lieu of S. 372), which included public funding in presidential and congressional primary and general elections.[45] As reported with only one dissenting vote, S. 3044 created a system for all federal elections, which is still in place in presidential elections: a voluntary system, with matching funds in the primaries and a fixed subsidy in the general election, all funded from the checkoff on federal tax returns.[46] The committee report expressed the view then in ascendancy about the need for public funding:

The only way in which Congress can eliminate reliance on large private contributions and still ensure adequate presentation to the electorate of competing candidates is through comprehensive public financing.... The election of federal officials is not a private affair. It is the foundation of our government. As Senator Mansfield recently observed, it is now clear that "we shall not finally come to grips with the problems except as we are prepared to pay for the public business of elections with public funds."[47]

Senate debate on S. 3044 lasted for 13 days, in which proponents were able to defeat four amendments to drop public financing completely, two amendments to reduce the level of public funds, one amendment to reduce funding to incumbents by 30%, and one amendment to add three free mass mailings to general election candidates. The Senate passed S. 3044 on April 11, 1974, by a 53-32 vote,[48] following a second, and successful, vote to invoke cloture. (See Appendix 1 for details on this measure.)

Public financing of congressional elections, however, was not included in the House Administration Committee's reported version of the 1974 FECA Amendments, H.R. 16090. Supporters, led by Representatives John Anderson and Morris Udall, attempted to add a voluntary matching system for House and Senate general elections, but their amendment to H.R. 16090 was defeated by a 187-228 vote.[49] Public financing of congressional elections was a particularly contentious issue in the House-Senate conference on S. 3044, but ultimately it was dropped, while the presidential public financing provisions were left intact. That bill did, however, leave spending limits (without public funding) in place for congressional elections, at different levels than in S. 3044 initially: $70,000 for House primaries and general elections, the greater of eight cents per eligible voter, or $100,000, in Senate primaries, and the greater of 12 cents per eligible voter, or $150,000, in Senate general elections.[50] Also, limits on spending from personal and family resources were imposed on House candidates ($25,000) and Senate candidates ($35,000).[51]

94th Congress (1975-1976)

Activity on behalf of public financing of congressional elections subsided considerably after the 93rd Congress, which had seen particularly strong momentum for governmental and electoral reforms as the Watergate scandal was unfolding. Public finance supporters did, however, make several unsuccessful attempts to revive the issue in the 94th through 96th Congresses.

During consideration of the FECA Amendments of 1976 in the 94th Congress, Senate supporters of public financing failed to get congressional public financing included in the bill reported by the Rules and

Administration Committee (S. 3065). House supporters, led by Representative Phil Burton, offered a floor amendment to the FECA Amendments (H.R. 12406), providing for matching funds in House and Senate general elections; the amendment failed on a 121-274 vote.[52]

95th Congress (1977-1978)

The 95th Congress began auspiciously for public finance supporters with the announced support of House Speaker Thomas P. O'Neill, Jr., and Senate Majority Leader Robert Byrd, with the elevation of public finance supporter Frank Thompson to House Administration chairman, and with a series of election reform measures, including public financing of congressional elections, by President Jimmy Carter.

The Senate Rules and Administration Committee considered S. 926, which, as introduced by Senators Kennedy, Dick Clark, Alan Cranston, Charles Mathias, and Russell Schweicker, proposed matching funds in Senate primaries and a combination of subsidies and matching funds in Senate general elections. The reported version of S. 926, however, deleted funding for primary elections, as suggested by sponsors, in order to increase chances for passage in the House.[53] Opposition to public financing was strong enough to force three cloture votes to limit debate on S. 926. After the final cloture vote failed, the Senate voted 58-39 for an amendment by Senator James Allen to delete public financing of Senate general elections.[54]

The new House leadership support led to six days of House Administration Committee hearings on public financing of congressional elections, although no consensus developed over what approach to choose.[55] An attempt to report a bill for partial public funding of House general elections failed in October 1977, after approval of two amendments offered by public finance opponents which added to the costs of the system and were seen as making the bill more difficult to pass (one extended funding to primaries; the other extended funding to all candidates who met a contribution threshold). Following adoption of these amendments, Chairman Thompson discontinued the markup, saying the votes were lacking to report a measure.[56]

On two occasions during the second session of the 95th Congress, the House narrowly defeated rules to allow consideration of public finance measures. An amendment to H.R. 11315, intended as a non-controversial set of amendments to federal campaign finance law, was offered in March 1978 by Representatives Thomas Foley and Barber Conable, proposing a matching fund system in House general elections. The underlying bill became embroiled in controversy, however, thus poisoning the atmosphere for House consideration of the public finance amendment as well.[57] The open rule, allowing for consideration of the Foley-Conable amendment, was defeated on a 198-209 vote on March 21, 1978.[58] Included in those voting against the rule were some 25 Republicans who had reportedly committed to voting for the public finance amendment.[59]

A second effort by public finance supporters came with a proposed amendment to the Federal Election Commission (FEC) authorization bill for FY1979 (H.R. 11983). The amendment, similar to the one offered in March 1978, was offered by Representatives Foley, Conable, Anderson, and Abner Mikva. In contrast with the situation in March, the reported rule was a closed one, thus prohibiting amendments on the floor. An effort to defeat the proposed rule was made by public finance supporters, but it failed on a 213-196 vote on July 19, 1978.[60] That vote, which observers saw as reflecting congressional sentiment on public financing, ended consideration of the issue for the 95th Congress.

96th Congress (1979-1980)

As the 96th Congress began, the House leadership accorded the efforts of public finance advocates — led by Representatives Foley, Conable, Anderson, Udall, Mikva, and Tim Wirth — priority status by designating their proposal H.R. 1. Similar to the failed amendments of the 95th Congress, the bill provided for matching funds in House general elections, in conjunction with voluntary spending limits. The House Administration Committee held five days of hearings in March 1979 on this and other public finance bills.[61] On May 24, 1979, despite efforts by supporters to gain more support, the bill failed to be reported, on a 8-17 vote.[62] With that vote, the momentum for extending public financing to congressional elections that had begun in the 93rd Congress came to an end.

97th – 99th Congresses (1981-1986)

While public financing remained an objective for many in Congress and bills continued to be introduced, the 97th through 99th Congresses saw no concerted effort in pursuit of this goal. In part, this reflected a changed political environment, with Senate control during this period (1981-1987) shifting to Republicans, generally less supportive of public financing than Democrats, and with frustration over the failure to enact public financing in the 93rd through 96th Congresses. Those advocating campaign finance reform set their sights on a less sweeping goal during the 1980s, and much of the 1990s: restricting the growing role of political action committees (PACs), the political agents of interest groups, in the financing of congressional elections. Like public financing, curbs on PACs were intended to lessen the importance of money, particularly "interested" money, in elections. Unlike public financing, restrictions on PACs did not involve the highly controversial issue of using tax revenues to fund campaigns and the invariably associated goal of limits on campaign spending. But, despite 19 days of hearings in the 97th through 99th Congresses, partisan stalemate on the PAC issue kept any major campaign finance bills from floor votes.[63]

100th Congress (1987-1988)

The political environment again shifted in the 100th Congress, with a Democratic majority in the Senate following the 1986 elections. With this change, the goal of campaign reform advocates quickly extended from curbs on PACs to their longer-standing objective of public financing and campaign spending limits in congressional elections. The twin ideas of voluntary spending limits and participation incentives in the form of public funds or some form of cost-saving benefits became the cornerstone of the leading reform proposals through the 105th Congress.

On the first day of the 100th Congress, Senate Majority Leader Robert Byrd joined Senator David Boren in cosponsoring S. 2, which became the focus of reform efforts and eventually gained 50 additional cosponsors. As reported by the Rules and Administration Committee, the bill featured public funding for Senate general election candidates who agreed to spending limits (in both their primary and general election campaigns) and aggregate PAC receipts limits for House and Senate candidates.[64] The public funding amount for major party candidates was equal to 80% of the state's spending limit for the general election. The measure was brought to the floor in June 1987, in the face of strong Republican opposition and the stated intention of opponents to filibuster the measure. After a failed vote to invoke cloture, sponsors of S. 2 offered an amendment to change the public funding component from a full subsidy for major party candidates to a matching fund system, thereby reducing in half the cost of the subsidy (and changing the expenditure limit formula as well). Opponents were not mollified, and four successive cloture votes in June 1987 also failed.

Sponsors made yet another attempt to scale back the public funds component of the bill, in an effort to gain the needed votes to overcome the filibuster. The second substitute amendment provided subsidies only to those whose opponents exceeded the voluntary limits, as both a disincentive to the large spender and as a means of "leveling the playing field." In addition, the substitute offered lower postal and broadcast rates to candidates who agreed to abide by the voluntary spending limits, both as an incentive to participation in the system and as a means of curbing campaign costs. This change also proved insufficient to ameliorate the opposition, and, following three additional failed cloture votes, the measure was pulled from further consideration in February 1988.[65]

101st Congress (1989-1990)

House and Senate leaders offered and enabled passage of bills featuring spending limits and public benefits (the concept of public financing per se became broadened to public benefits as Members sought ways to reduce the level of direct treasury funding to campaigns). The Senate Rules and Administration Committee reported S. 137 (Boren-Mitchell), based on the final version of S. 2 in the 100th Congress, with spending limits, public benefits, and a PAC receipts cap.[66] A substitute was offered May 11, 1990, reflecting several features aimed at increasing support for a public benefits and spending limits system. Public funds per se, in the form of direct cash payments to candidates, were to be triggered only on a contingency basis, to compensate participating candidates against free-spending opponents and independent expenditures against them (or for their opponents). The principal subsidy for all participants was to take the form of broadcast communication vouchers, whereby broadcasters would be reimbursed with federal funds but no funds would be transmitted directly to candidates. The other benefits were a reduced broadcast rate, through requiring the lowest unit rate be made available only to participating candidates (and making such time not subject to preemption), and a reduced postal rate; neither of these benefits involved direct payments to candidates although the postal benefit did involve revenue loss to the U.S. Postal Service. Even the spending limits, based on the same population-based formula as was used in the 100th Congress bill, were adjusted as a means of increasing Senate support, with the provision for an additional 25% in allowable spending from small in-state donors.

Senate debate began July 30, 1990, and encompassed 16 roll-call votes on amendments, including one by Senator Mitch McConnell to strike public funds entirely (defeated by 46-49)[67] and another by Senator John Kerry to greatly increase the level of public funds (defeated by 38-60).[68] On August 1, 1990, the Senate passed S. 137 on a 59-40 vote, with five Republicans for and only one Democrat against. It featured voluntary Senate spending limits, communication vouchers, postal and broadcast discounts, and subsidies to match independent expenditures and wealthy opponents, plus other campaign finance provisions.[69] (See Appendix 1 for details on this measure.)

In the House, the Democratic leadership offered a measure which went even further than the Senate bill in reducing the role of public funds as an incentive to adhering to spending limits. In exchange for agreeing to spending limits, which were set at $550,000 for a two-year election cycle (and an additional $165,000 in the case of a nominee who won a competitive primary), H.R. 5400 (Swift) offered House general election candidates three benefits, none of which involved direct payments to candidates. These included lower rates on first- and third-class mailings in the last 90 days of an election, one free radio or TV spot for every two purchased, and a 100% tax credit for in-state contributors (up to $50, or $100 on joint returns). While public funding was involved in H.R. 5400, it took a less direct form than with candidate subsidies. H.R. 5400 was passed by the House on August 3, 1990, by a 255-155 vote.[70] (See Appendix 1 for details on this measure.)

A conference committee was appointed, but, faced with large differences between H.R. 5400 and S. 137 and a presidential veto, it never met.

102nd Congress (1991-1992)

Public financing of congressional elections advanced further in the legislative process during the 102nd Congress than ever before or since. Bills comparable to those passed in the 101st Congress were approved by the Senate and House and reconciled in conference, but vetoed by President George H.W. Bush.

On March 20, 1991, the Senate Rules and Administration Committee reported S. 3 (Mitchell-Boren), similar to S. 137 (101st Congress).[71] When

Senate debate began May 15, the Boren substitute amendment was incorporated into S. 3. Debate took place over six days and encompassed 21 roll-call amendment votes, including one by Senator McConnell to eliminate the public funding and spending limits from the bill (defeated on a 42-56 vote)[72] and one by Senator Kerry to increase vastly the public funding level in the bill (defeated on a 39-58 vote).[73] On May 23, 1991, the Senate passed S. 3 on a 56-42 vote, with all but five Republicans voting against and all but five Democrats in favor.[74] As passed, S. 3 included voluntary Senate spending limits, an extra 25% allowance in spending from small in-state donations, broadcast communication vouchers, broadcast and postal discounts, and conditional subsidies to match non-complying opponents and independent expenditures.[75] (See Appendix 1 for details on this measure.)

The House Administration Committee's Task Force on Campaign Finance Reform led to a Democratic bill, H.R. 3750 (Gejdenson), reported by the committee on November 12, 1991,[76] and amended by the Rules Committee on November 23.[77] The bill replaced the free TV and radio time and the tax credit in the 101st Congress bill with a matching fund system, while leaving some form of reduced mailing rates. But concerns over perceived unpopularity of public funding led sponsors to omit provisions to finance benefits, beyond allowing voluntary contributions to the Make Democracy Work Fund, in the version brought to the House floor.[78] The House passed H.R. 3750 on November 25, 1991, by a 273-156 vote.[79] As passed, it featured voluntary House spending limits, in exchange for matching funds and lower postal rates, with extra spending for runoffs or close primaries and extra matching funds to offset non-complying opponents and independent expenditures.[80] (See Appendix 1 for details on this measure.)

A conference committee was appointed to reconcile the two passed bills and filed its report April 3, 1992 (amended on April 8).[81] The conference bill combined features of S. 3 and H.R. 3750, leaving House and Senate spending limits and public benefits largely intact for their own candidates. Major changes in the conference version centered around other issues, such as PAC contribution limits, soft money, and bundling.[82] The conference also delayed implementation of the spending limits and public funding systems pending enactment of a funding mechanism. (See Appendix 1 for details on this measure.) The House passed the conference report on April 9 by a 259-165 vote.[83] The Senate followed suit on April 30 with a 58-42 vote.[84] President Bush, citing his opposition to spending limits and public financing, vetoed the bill May 9.[85] On May 13, a Senate override vote failed by 57-42, thus ending debate on the issue for the 102nd Congress.[86]

103rd Congress (1993-1994)

At the start of the 103rd Congress, Democratic leaders introduced bills identical to those in the 102nd Congress: H.R. 3 (Gejdenson) and S. 3 (Boren). With a President of the same party in favor, 1993 reform prospects seemed improved.

On March 18, 1993, the Senate Rules and Administration Committee reported S. 3 (largely the bill vetoed in 1992, including the House provisions).[87] Prior to the Senate debate, President William J. Clinton made his own recommendations on May 7, 1993, which added such provisions to the vetoed 102nd Congress bill as congressional broadcast vouchers and an increased tax checkoff financed by an end to lobbying expense deductions.[88]

On May 21, Senate began debate on a leadership substitute to the committee version of S. 3, focused solely on Senate elections and reflecting the Clinton proposal and a federal PAC ban. Debate lasted for three weeks, encompassing three cloture votes and 24 recorded amendment votes. The filibuster was not broken until agreement was reached between Democratic leaders and seven Republicans to add the Durenberger/Exon Amendment. This provision dropped the bill's broadcast vouchers, allowed subsidies only to offset independent spending and spending in excess of the limits by non-complying opponents, and repealed the exempt function income exclusion on principal campaign committees of candidates who exceeded spending limits (in effect, subjecting them to a 34% tax on income).[89] Passage of this amendment cleared the way for a successful vote to invoke cloture and passage of S. 3 the next day on a 60-38 vote.[90] (See Appendix 1 for details on this measure.)

The House leadership bill, H.R. 3, was reported from the House Administration Committee on November 10, 1993, as amended by the committee and focused only on House elections.[91] The reported bill featured voluntary House spending limits and communication vouchers (based on matching donations); other than contingency funds to compensate for non-complying opponents and independent expenditures, no other benefits were offered. After defeating a rule to allow votes on more alternatives, the House, on November 22, 1993, passed H.R. 3 by 255-175.[92] (See Appendix 1 for details on this measure.)

House and Senate compromise efforts were impeded by differences on PAC limits and funding sources; both bills avoided establishing a funding mechanism for the public benefits, deferring implementation until revenue legislation could be enacted. Late in the second session, on September 29,

1994, Democratic leaders announced a deal, but Senate Republicans led a filibuster against appointing conferees, ending with a failed cloture vote (52-46) on September 30, 1994.[93]

104th – 110th Congresses (1995-2007)

The shift to Republican control of the House and Senate in 1995 effectively killed the momentum for public financing in Congress, given generally strong Republican opposition to both public financing and spending limits. Public finance bills continued to be introduced in every Congress, including in the 104th when Senators John McCain and Russell Feingold introduced their first campaign finance reform bill, establishing themselves as the Senate's leading reform advocates. That bill (S. 1219) was the successor to the bills passed in the previous three Congresses, and it reflected the same pre-1996 consensus among campaign finance reform advocates that prioritized curbing the high cost of congressional elections and replacing private funds with other funding sources.

The election of 1996 proved to be a watershed in the campaign finance debate, as largely unregulated campaign activity (party soft money and election-related issue advocacy) seemed to overshadow the regulated activity. In response, the leading reform advocates in Congress made significant changes in their proposed legislation at the start of the 105th Congress. S. 25 (McCain-Feingold), as well as its companion H.R. 493 (Shays-Meehan), added provisions to the comparable 104th Congress bills to allow federal regulation of election-related activity then being conducted as "issue advocacy." Following the most intensive congressional activity on campaign finance reform since the 1970s, a revised S. 25 was offered in the fall of 1997, featuring provisions on party soft money and issue advocacy. What was striking was that the provisions on congressional spending limits and public benefits, and on PACs, the key elements of reformers' objectives for at least the previous 10 years, were eliminated from the bill entirely. Thus, in one year's time, the very nature of the campaign finance debate had shifted from efforts to *improve* the existing regulatory system to efforts to *save* it from becoming meaningless in the face of newly emerging campaign practices. This debate, in the wake of the 1996 elections, was to last until 2002, when BCRA, commonly known as McCain-Feingold, was enacted.

109th Congress Bills

Appendix 2 contains summaries of the four public finance bills introduced in the 109th Congress. All were House bills, dealing only with House elections. Two of the bills — H.R. 2753 (Andrews) and H.R. 4694 (Obey) — would have provided public funding only in the general election. The Andrews bill would have provided up to $750,000 (based on media costs in the district) to candidates who met certain criteria, such as a $100 limit on individual donations and an 80% in-state funding requirement; but, unlike others introduced, the bill would have imposed no spending limit. The Obey bill would have established a mandatory spending limit, based on the median household income in the district, and would have provided public funds to equal those limits. The benefit would have been financed in part by a tax on corporate income. The bill provided for fast-track consideration of a constitutional amendment to allow mandatory spending limits if the limits in the bill were struck down.

The other two bills — H.R. 3099 (Tierney) and H.R. 5281 (Leach) — would have offered benefits in both primary and general elections. The Leach bill would have provided funds to match contributions from in-state contributors and would have imposed a $500,000 per election spending limit. The Tierney bill was the Clean Money, Clean Elections measure, which would have provided public subsidies equal to the spending limit in the primary and general election, specified allotments of free broadcast time, and additional broadcast time at 50% of the lowest unit rate. Candidates would have qualified by raising specified numbers of small donations. (The clean money model is discussed in greater detail under the States' Experience section of this report.)

110th Congress Bills

As of this writing, four bills that would provide public congressional campaign financing have been introduced in the 110th Congress. H.R. 1614 (Tierney), S. 936 (Durbin), and S. 1285 (Durbin) are similar, but the House and Senate bills also feature important differences. H.R. 2817 (Obey) contains some of the same characteristics of H.R. 1614, S. 936, and S. 1285, but does not appear to be based on the "clean money, clean elections" model found in the former three bills. Appendix 3 at the end of this report reviews major provisions of each bill.

H.R. 1614, S. 936, and S. 1285 all include hallmarks frequently associated with "clean elections" programs, such as full public financing for participating candidates, a "seed money" period in which candidates would demonstrate viability by raising small start-up contributions, and additional funds for participating candidates facing non-participating opponents or attacks by outside groups. The most notable difference between the House and Senate bills is that they would all cover only one chamber. H.R. 1614 would apply only to House candidates; S. 936 and S. 1285 would apply only to Senate candidates. S. 936 and S. 1285 are identical except for one provision regarding tax credits. Although Section 112 of S. 936 would authorize a $500 tax credit for citizen contributions to the proposed Senate public financing fund, S. 1285 contains no such provision. Similarly, although S. 936 was referred to the Senate Finance Committee, S. 1285 was referred to the Senate Committee on Rules and Administration.

H.R. 1614 is similar to its predecessor, H.R. 3099 (described above), which Representative Tierney introduced in the 109th Congress. Unlike the 109th Congress version of the bill, H.R. 1614 would authorize tax credits for contributions to the House Clean Elections Fund (the proposed depository for public funds for House campaigns) and create a Clean Elections Review Commission to regularly review the functioning of the House public financing system and make legislative recommendations. The Clean Elections Review Commission would not replace the FEC. (By contrast, H.R. 3099 proposed restructuring the FEC.) H.R. 1614 would supplement the base public financing allocation for participating candidates by an index of media costs in the state in which the candidate was running.

Much of the language in S. 936 and S. 1285 is similar to that found in H.R. 1614, including proposed benefits to candidates, candidate eligibility, "seed money" mechanisms allowing for private initial fundraising, and availability of additional "fair fight" funds to counter spending by opposing candidates or outside groups. S. 936 and S. 1285 include a debate requirement for publicly funded candidates — a provision not contained in H.R. 1614. Permissible civil penalties for excessive contributions or expenditures would be higher in H.R. 1614 than those authorized in S. 936 and S. 1285. Each bill establishes a similarly structured commission to review the functioning of proposed public financing programs. S. 936 and S. 1285 authorize expedited Senate review of the Fair Elections Review Commission's legislative recommendations; H.R. 1614 does not contain a similar provision. All three bills would limit the amount of party coordinated expenditures that may be made on behalf of publicly financed candidates. H.R. 1614 (but not S. 936 or S. 1285) would also establish a broad definition of "payment made in coordination with a candidate," as summarized in Appendix 3.

H.R. 1614, S. 936, and S. 1285 also propose slightly different thresholds for qualifying contributions that would trigger disbursement of public funds. H.R. 1614 proposes a fixed number of minimum contributions for major-party candidates, while S. 936 and S. 1285 base their threshold on a formula accounting for the number of congressional districts in the state. Similarly, the House and Senate bills propose different methods for formulating the base public funding allocation for major candidates. For House candidates, under H.R. 1614 the base allocation would be the national average of expenditures by winning House candidates in the past two election cycles, as adjusted by an index of media markets for the state in which the candidate was running. For Senate candidates (per S. 936 and S. 1285), the base would be $750,000 plus $150,000 for each congressional district (in excess of 1 district) in the state in which the candidate was running. The base would be adjusted based on media markets in the state (an index to be determined by the FEC and the Federal Communications Commission) and biannually based on the consumer price index.

H.R. 1614 proposes to fund public financing through appropriations, unspent seed money, public financing penalty amounts, and similar resources, including tax incentives for public donations to the fund. The Senate fund proposed in S. 936 would rely on many of the same revenue sources specified in H.R. 1614, although unlike the House bill, the Senate program would receive revenues from spectrum user fees and "proceeds from recovered spectrum [auctions]."[94] As noted previously, although S. 936 would provide tax incentives for public donations to the public financing fund, S. 1285 would not do so.

The three bills also differ regarding support for broadcast communications. Although H.R. 1614 would provide free broadcast time to publicly financed candidates, S. 936 and S. 1285 would provide political advertising vouchers to participating candidates. S. 936 and S. 1285 specify that candidates may, for cash value, transfer their right to all or portions of their vouchers to party committees. Under all three bills, publicly financed candidates could purchase additional time below the lowest unit charge (LUC). The House bill would reduce charges to publicly financed candidates to 50% of the LUC, while the Senate bills would reduce that rate to 80% of the LUC. H.R. 1614 would deny the LUC to non-participating candidates; S. 936 and S. 1285 do not specify such a provision.

Whereas the other three 110th Congress bills (and most public financing proposals) would make public financing *voluntary*, H.R. 2817 (Obey) would require House candidates to participate in public financing during the general election.[95]

Although H.R. 2817 does not compel participation in public financing per se, it would require that candidates observe spending limits and make expenditures only from a proposed public financing fund. The only other permissible source of candidate funding would be state and national party contributions of up to 5% of the candidate's spending limit. The bill would also ban independent expenditures and "soft money" spending in House elections. H.R. 2817 specifies expedited procedures[96] for congressional consideration of a constitutional amendment if the Supreme Court found any part of the bill unconstitutional.[97]

H.R. 2817 proposes general-election spending limits based on median household income in the congressional district, with a maximum of $2 million in the wealthiest district. For major-party candidates, actual spending limits would be adjusted by the ratio of the vote major-party candidates received in the three most recent general elections in that district. For example, of a $2 million maximum, if the average Republican vote share in the district in the three most recent elections were 55%, compared with 45% for Democrats, a publicly financed Republican candidate could spend $1.1 million (55% of $2 million), while a publicly financed Democrat could spend the remaining $900,000 (45% of $2 million). Candidates in other districts (the non-wealthiest) could spend lesser amounts based on a similar formula specified in the bill. Candidates could increase their spending limits by submitting specified numbers of petition signatures. The FEC would be charged with distributing public funds (from a proposed Grassroots Good Citizenship Fund) equal to specified spending limits. The bill specifies that voluntary taxpayer contributions from refunds owed, other voluntary contributions, and a 0.1% tax on corporate income exceeding $10 million would fund public financing. The FEC would be required to launch an extensive public education campaign regarding public financing; that program would rely at least in part on broadcasting time provided by television networks. Finally, H.R. 2817 contains "sunset" language specifying that the bill's provisions would expire in 2022. Congress could alter that time frame through legislation.

To summarize, all four bills propose comprehensive public financing programs, but do so in different ways. H.R. 2817 (Obey) proposes perhaps the most direct change to the status quo because it would make public financing mandatory in general elections. By contrast, candidates operating under the other three bills could choose to participate in public financing — and would have to meet specific criteria to do so — or could rely on traditional, private campaign financing. H.R. 1614, S. 936, and S. 1285 explicitly propose public financing for primary elections. The public financing program proposed in H.R. 2817 would only cover general elections, but the bill also specifies spending limits for primary elections. H.R. 2817 would ban independent expenditures in House elections. By contrast, H.R. 1614, S. 936, would provide "fair fight funds" designed to counter high-spending opponents and those airing independent expenditures against participating candidates or in favor of their opponents. Essentially, while H.R. 2817 would replace the private campaign financing system in general elections, H.R. 1614, S. 936, and S. 1285 propose a benefits package designed to allow publicly financed candidates to compete within the current system.

As of this writing, only S. 1285 has received a hearing during the 110th Congress. On June 20, 2007, the Senate Committee on Rules and Administration heard testimony on the bill from Senators, a former FEC chairman, and interest group representatives. At that hearing, Senators Durbin and Specter (and former senator Warren Rudman) testified in favor of the bill, saying that it was a "modest" step toward reducing the role of money in elections and a means to restoring public trust in government. In particular, Senator Durbin emphasized what he called an "unsustainable" current system of private fundraising that potentially separates lawmakers from average voters and distracts them from policymaking. Minority Leader McConnell testified against the bill, citing declining public participation in the presidential public financing system and philosophical opposition to public financing for politicians. Chairman Feinstein and Ranking Member Bennett both expressed concerns at the hearing about the possibility of "fringe" candidates receiving public funds. In a letter to committee members, the National Association of Broadcasters (NAB) expressed "great concern" about proposed LUC reductions for participating candidates and sections of S. 1285 that would bar broadcasters from preempting candidate advertising and fund public financing through spectrum usage fees.[98]

DEVISING A CONGRESSIONAL PUBLIC FINANCE SYSTEM: OPTIONS FOR POLICYMAKERS

Based on the previous discussion of proposals that advanced in the legislative process, one can see the wide range of features that any public finance proposal might embody. This section enumerates some of the basic options facing Congress in any consideration of such proposals. (Further potential considerations for congressional public financing are discussed in the conclusion of this report. These considerations are based in part on experiences in the states, which are discussed in the following section.) CRS takes no position on any of the options presented here.

Setting Expenditure Limits

Establishing the limits on campaign expenditures is perhaps the thorniest aspect of devising a public financing system. It has become widely accepted in the political science community that, to the extent that high spending in elections reflects a desirable level of competitiveness, low spending limits can inhibit real competition.[99] In other words, low spending limits may reduce the chances for lesser known candidates to defeat candidates with higher visibility and name recognition. It was this principle that has often led public finance and spending limit proposals to be labeled by critics as "incumbent protection" measures, because incumbents typically start elections with much higher visibility than their challengers.

Spending limits for House campaigns have almost always been a specified across-the-board amount ($600,000 in the last bill to pass the House, in 1993), whereas the Senate limits have generally reflected a population-based formula. As late as 1997 when the initial McCain-Feingold bill was offered in the 105th Congress, the formula in Senate elections was essentially the same one incorporated into S. 2 (the leadership substitute) in the 100th Congress (in a general election — the lesser of: (a) $5.5 million, or (b) the greater of (i) $950,000, or (ii) $400,000, plus 30 cents times the voting age population (VAP), up to 4 million, and 25 cents times the VAP over 4 million; in a primary — 67% of general election limit, up to $2.75 million; and for a runoff — 20% of the general election limit).

The challenge for policymakers is to choose a spending limit that takes into account the realities of today's campaigns, allowing sufficient opportunity for a genuine competition which serves the public's interest. One way to offset potential damage to the vibrancy of the electoral process resulting from too stringent limits would be to increase the generosity of public funds and benefits, to lessen the need for both raising and spending money.

Coverage: General Elections Only or Primary Elections, Too?

While the bills that advanced in the 1970s included public funds in the primaries, most measures in more recent Congresses have covered only general elections. This has been the case not so much because the sponsors have not favored such coverage but more because of strategic decisions about the reduced likelihood of enacting a more complicated and more expensive system. Some have stated that they would settle for public funding in general elections for now and hopefully later return to the primary issue after some experience with a general election system. To some, however, the lack of inclusion of primaries may represent a serious flaw in recent proposals, with the prospect of private money entering the electoral system earlier and expenditures aimed at influencing the general election made during primaries, all to evade the restrictions of the general election system.[100] The bills debated in the 100th — 103rd Congresses incorporated the concept of providing benefits only in the general election but conditioning those benefits on adherence to voluntary spending limits in the primary as well as the general election.

Conditions for Receipt of Public Benefits

Invariably, proposals condition receipt of benefits on adherence to voluntary spending limits, whether solely in the election where the benefits are offered or in the primary as well as the general election. Most also require candidates to limit spending from personal and immediate family funds to a specified amount (generally applicable to loans as well). Some bills have added a requirement that candidates participate in a specified number of debates, and bills that passed in the 1990s added the requirement that broadcast ads must include closed-captioning. There is considerable latitude in what conditions may be imposed on candidates participating in this voluntary system.

Qualifying Requirements

In addition to requiring adherence to spending limits, proposals typically have some sort of qualifying requirement to prove a candidate is "serious" (i.e., that he or she has some degree of public support). Most often, the qualifying requirement is a fundraising threshold, comprising relatively small donations from a specified number of voters in that jurisdiction. Petition signatures is another option.

Public Funds: Matching Funds or Fixed Subsidies?

This choice may be informed by the experience the nation has had under the presidential system for the past 30 years, in which matching funds are available in the primaries and fixed subsidies are offered to candidates in the general election. As is discussed in the next section, the states also use a mix of these two forms of subsidies.

Fixed subsidies offer the advantage of simplicity and providing candidates greater ability to plan their campaigns, but, depending on the percentage of the spending limit the grant is intended to constitute, it can result in a much greater cost (in the presidential system, for example, major candidates in the general election get a subsidy equal to the spending limit). The matching fund approach would generally be less expensive and would offer the advantage of linking the receipt of public money with a demonstration of voter appeal by the candidate. Matching fund systems may offer the advantage of avoiding complex legislative or regulatory judgments about who is and is not a "serious" candidate, with the meeting of fundraising thresholds and the continuing raising of small donations considered an adequate means of so doing. If a matching fund system is preferred, there is also the consideration of whether funds should match contributions on an equal basis or a higher percentage (some bills have proposed a two- or three-to-one match, at least in some circumstances).

Public Benefits Other Than Direct Subsidies to Candidates

Whereas the bills that advanced in Congress during the post-Watergate 1970s were based on either direct subsidies or matching funds, the most prominent measures of the late 1980s and early 1990s reflected a move away from direct public funding to candidates. Instead, those bills featured either more indirect forms of public funding or cost-reducing benefits that did not involve public funds at all. These indirect public funding and public benefits measures, often designed to increase chances for passage in the face of perceived public opposition to use of public funds in elections, offer additional ideas in structuring a spending limits and public benefits package.

Indirect Public Funding

Several ideas have gained support in Congress at various times that make use of public funds in ways other than direct payments from the U.S. Treasury to the candidates, including the following:

- Tax credits for contributions to candidates abiding by limits — This could provide a grassroots fundraising incentive to candidates who agree to limit their expenditures. Most commonly, this takes the form of a 100% tax credit for contributions to participating candidates. Such a form of public funding is determined by citizens' decisions at the grassroots level, rather than decisions of a government agency, which supporters see as an important advantage. Presumably, the prospect of raising small donations much more easily would provide sufficient incentive for candidates to agree to limit spending. Most observers of the political system argue that the best kind of political money is that from individual citizens in small amounts. (It should be noted that from 1972-1986, the federal government allowed tax deductions or credits for political contributions, but they were eliminated as part of overall tax reform; also, many states have such incentives applicable to contributions in their elections.)

- Broadcast vouchers to candidates — The single largest component of the typical campaign budget (at least for statewide and national offices) and the biggest single factor in the rise of campaign costs in recent years has been broadcast advertising. Proposals have been advanced whereby candidates would be allocated specified amounts of broadcast vouchers, for which broadcasters would be reimbursed from the federal treasury. Under this plan, public monies do not get distributed directly to candidates, thus at least ostensibly avoiding some of the objections to public financing per se while focusing on what many consider the biggest single problem in campaign financing — the high cost of media. However, the mechanics of implementing such a plan, particularly in districts served by high density, high-cost media markets, pose potential concerns in terms of fairness and the particulars of individual campaigns.

- Lower postal rates for candidates abiding by limits — Another proposal which seeks to draw candidates into acceptance of campaign spending limits is one which offers participating candidates lower postal rates, such as those currently available to political party committees. This proposal involves public funds, but only indirectly, because the U.S. Postal Service would have to be reimbursed for revenue forgone as a result of its implementation. It is not clear to what extent a lower postal rate may serve as an inducement to candidates to limit spending, since postage is not a large component in a typical campaign budget, although it may well be more important in House than Senate races (especially in high-density media markets where media costs are seen as often prohibitively expensive). Lower postal rates do offer the advantage of acting to reduce campaign costs, generally seen as a worthwhile goal, regardless of one's position on spending limits or public financing.

Public Benefits without Public Funds

Proposals that passed in the 101st — 103rd Congresses (and the Senate-passed version of the BCRA (McCain-Feingold) in the 107th Congress) looked to broadcasters to offer some of the incentive toward candidate participation. Because of broadcasters' public interest obligations as part of their license agreements, sponsors sought to require broadcasters to offer lower rates to candidates participating in public funding, as a condition of their licenses and at no cost to the U.S. treasury. (On the basis of this principle, the federal government has since 1972 required broadcasters to charge political candidates at the lowest unit rate (LUR) available to commercial advertisers for the same time and class of advertising time.) Some proposals have gone beyond requiring still-lower rates to requiring broadcasters to provide specified amounts of free time to participating candidates. To the extent that these costs are removed from candidates, the overall cost of elections could be significantly curbed, which, as with lower postal rates, would appeal to many observers regardless of their views on spending limits and public financing. Yet such proposals invariably invite strong opposition from the broadcast industry. While the Senate version of BCRA in the 107th Congress offered substantial reductions in broadcast rates to candidates, this provision was removed in the House on a floor amendment.

Protecting Participants from Free-Spending Opponents and Outside Groups. One concept present in most bills offered since the 100th Congress but absent from the presidential system is protection offered to candidates who participate in public financing but are faced with large expenditures by nonparticipating opponents or are targeted in independent expenditures from outside groups. Most commonly, provisions designed to remedy such situations would

- increase spending limits on participants to match expenditures by opponents in excess of the spending limits and by independent expenditures in amounts above a specified level; and/or
- provide participants with additional public funds to match excessive spending from non-participating opponents or for opposing independent expenditures, perhaps with a cap on overall funds provided in this circumstance.

Providing additional funds, or allowing for supplementary private funding, to participating candidates facing non-participating opponents offers protection against being greatly outspent and presumably would deter candidates considering forgoing public financing. A potential problem with these disincentives is the increased costs they would add to a public funding system, costs not easily predictable. What has not been reflected in recent proposals but may have to be addressed in future ones is the activity by outside groups (such as 527 political organizations) that spend money outside the purview of federal election law (i.e., soft money).

Other Disincentives Toward Non-Participation

While public finance bills have typically focused on offering benefits as an inducement toward agreeing to expenditure limits, more recent proposals have also looked to add disincentives as well, to impose some sort of penalty on candidates not participating in the system (beyond providing benefits to the participating opponent). These proposals appeal to those who would like to lessen the role of public funds but still wish to achieve meaningful levels of participation in the system. Critics see these proposals as heavy-handed measures designed to bludgeon candidates into participating, thus casting doubts on whether participation can fairly be deemed to be voluntary. Some of the disincentives advanced in recent years include the following:

- requiring a disclaimer on campaign advertisements of a candidate's non-participation — This provision, requiring non-participants to state in their ads that they do not abide by spending limits, was included in Senate bills passed in the 101st - 103rd Congresses;

- disallowing lowest unit rate requirement for non-participants —
  This provision, included in the 101st Congress Senate bill, as
  passed, would have removed the lowest unit rate requirement for
  candidates not participating in the system; and
- tax campaigns of non-participating candidates — Political
  campaigns are generally exempt from paying taxes on money
  raised.[101] The Senate bill passed in the 103rd Congress removed
  the exempt function income exclusion on principal campaign
  committees of candidates who exceeded spending limits, thus in
  effect subjecting those campaigns to a 34% tax.

Conditional Public Subsidies

One idea closely related to the proposals in the prior two sections is to
provide public funds only as a last resort, when a participant is faced by an
opponent who exceeded spending limits or by opposing independent
expenditures. As is explained in the "State Experiences" section that follows,
some states feature such a provision, aimed at curbing arguably excessive
campaign spending without incurring the expense to the taxpayers that most
public finance systems would incur. It would be applied on a very selective
basis and would presumably act as a strong inhibitor against only the most
excessive campaign spending. The Senate bill passed in the 103rd Congress
contained this feature, in addition to the direct incentives of lower postal and
broadcast rates.

Paying for Public Financing

Clearly, the decisions made about the aforementioned variables will
determine the cost of any public finance system. Estimates of costs of public
finance systems vary considerably, according to the details of the systems
envisioned. For bills considered in the 101st — 103rd Congresses, one can
look to the required Congressional Budget Office (CBO) cost estimates,
bearing in mind that the bills passed were often changed substantially from
those reported and for which estimates were provided. At the start of the
103rd Congress, the Senate Rules and Administration Committee reported S.
3, which was essentially the bill vetoed during the 102nd Congress and thus
contained provisions affecting both House and Senate elections. Benefits for
House elections consisted of matching funds (accounting for up to one-third

of the spending limit) and reduced mailing rates; Senate election benefits consisted of voter communication vouchers (of up to 20% of the general election limit), reduced mailing rates, and contingent public grants to compensate candidates opposed by free-spending opponents and by independent expenditures. CBO estimated that this rather modest system (in terms of level of public funds) would range in cost from $90 million to $175 million in the 1996 election cycle and from $95 million to $190 million in the 1998 election cycle.[102]

At the other extreme, the most generous proposal currently being advanced at both federal and state levels is the "Clean Money, Clean Elections" measure, advocated by interest group Public Campaign. H.R. 1614 (Tierney, 110th Congress), S. 936 (Durbin, 110th Congress), S. 1285 (Durbin 110th Congress), H.R. 3099 (Tierney, 109th Congress), and S. 719 (Wellstone, 107th Congress) are variations on the clean elections model and would (or would have) provide public funds in the primary and general elections; such funds are intended to lower all candidate spending in those elections. Public Campaign's website states,

> The cost of implementing such a system for Congressional elections is estimated to be less than a billion dollars per year out of a federal budget of close to two trillion dollars (that's about a half of a 10th of a percent of the federal budget: 0.05%). That amounts to less than $10 per-taxpayer, per-year. [103]

Thus, by Public Campaign's estimates, congressional elections would cost somewhat less than $2 billion every election cycle.

Most proposals since the mid-1970s have relied upon a tax checkoff, based on the presidential model, whereby taxpayers could designate a certain number of tax dollars to go into the fund to pay for congressional elections. This idea is intended to mitigate negative images that might arise from "taxpayer funding" of elections, because of the direct role provided citizens in the distribution of tax revenues. Because of those perceptions, however, the 101st — 103rd Congresses sought creative ways to offset any losses to the U.S. Treasury, or remained silent on funding sources, leaving those decisions to subsequent "enacting legislation." Proposals since that time have looked to such things as broadcast licensing fees, a tax on lobbyists, and a tax on corporate income to offset treasury losses.[104]

STATE EXPERIENCES WITH PUBLIC FINANCING

INTRODUCTION

State public financing programs emerged primarily in the 1970s, although a few states provided limited assistance to campaigns early in the 20th century.[105] Prior to the 1970s, many programs that did exist provided funding to political parties rather than directly to candidate campaigns. (As noted previously, political parties were historically the major funders of congressional campaigns, especially before the 1960s.) States vary considerably in whether they offer public financing, how they do so, and why.[106]

Currently, 16 states offer some form of direct public financing to candidates' campaigns (see Figure 1).[107] Of those, seven states fund only statewide races (Florida, Maryland, Michigan, New Mexico, North Carolina, Rhode Island, and Vermont). Nine states fund legislative *and* statewide races (Arizona, Connecticut, Hawaii, Maine, Massachusetts, Minnesota, Nebraska, New Jersey, and Wisconsin; see Figure 2), although which statewide campaigns are eligible for funding varies.

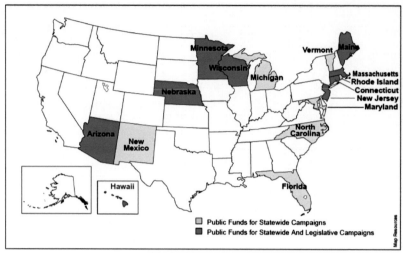

Source: CRS research on state public financing programs as discussed elswhere in this report (1/07)

Figure 1. States Offering Public Financing.

States have chosen two major public-financing frameworks. First, the clean money, clean elections model (hereafter, clean money) is a national initiative developed by an interest group and is designed to cover full campaign costs.[108] Clean money programs generally offer fixed subsidies to candidates once they meet basic qualifying requirements. All qualifying candidates receive the same amount of funding, which is, at least in theory, sufficient to cover all campaign costs.[109] All clean money programs are similar, with adaptations in each state (e.g., which offices are covered). Second, and in contrast to the clean money model, other state public financing mechanisms vary considerably. These programs are typically older, and developed more individually. Through matching funds and other benefits, these programs are designed to reduce the need for and impact from private fundraising, but are less likely than clean money programs to offer full public financing to participating candidates. States fund both approaches through a combination of tax checkoffs, direct appropriations from state legislatures, revenues from various fines and fees, and other sources. Additional details are discussed below.

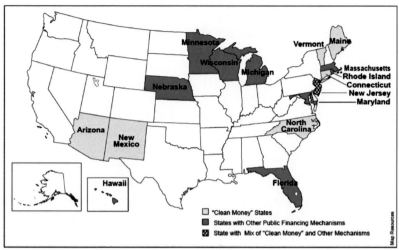

Source: CRS research on state public financing programs as discussed elsewhere in this report (1/07)

Figure 2. Types of Public Financing Offered in the States

TYPES OF PUBLIC FINANCING

As Table 1 and Figure 2 show, seven states offer some form of the clean money model of public financing. The clean money model offers full public financing to candidates who agree to certain restrictions, particularly spending limits. Candidates who agree to those restrictions, which vary by state, receive public funds via fixed subsidies. Specific amounts are determined by each state. The plan originated with the interest group Public Campaign, which describes itself as "a non-profit, nonpartisan organization dedicated to sweeping reform that aims to dramatically reduce the role of big special interest money in American politics."[110] The group advocates the clean money program at the local, state, and federal levels around the country. Currently, clean money programs in Arizona, Connecticut, Maine, New Jersey (a pilot legislative program), New Mexico, North Carolina, and Vermont offer public financing to the candidates for the offices noted in Table 1. Although all clean money programs are adapted to states' individual needs (e.g., different offices are covered in each state), the major components of the program are similar nationwide. All programs were approved by voters or state legislatures between 1997 and 2005. (During the 109th Congress, Representative John F. Tierney introduced H.R. 3099, which embodied a clean money model for House elections. During the 107th Congress, Senator Paul Wellstone introduced a similar bill, S. 719. Neither chamber took any action on the bills.)

By contrast, 10 states offer public financing through programs other than the clean money model: Hawaii, Florida, Nebraska, Maryland, Massachusetts, Michigan, Minnesota, New Jersey (gubernatorial campaigns), Rhode Island, and Wisconsin.[111] While the clean money system features a uniform model for public financing and is a relatively recent initiative, other public financing programs in the states vary widely. Many of the latter programs were initiated in the 1970s, in the Watergate aftermath. Some of the most notable differences between clean money models and other programs are how candidates receive public funding and how much money is available to those candidates. Although clean money funds are generally distributed through subsidies that allocate fixed amounts to candidates, states that employ other programs rely primarily on matching funds. The amount of matching funds candidates receive depends on the amount of private contributions raised. States generally match 100%, and sometimes more, of the amount a candidate raises through private contributions.

Whether clean money models or other systems, public financing programs do not guarantee unlimited funds. States generally limit the percentage of contributions that may be matched, or cap the total amount of funds that may be disbursed.[112] Available revenues often influence these decisions. For example, in Michigan, a tax checkoff system funds public financing for qualifying gubernatorial candidates. Just as in the presidential public-financing system, general-election funding in Michigan takes priority. Funding is first reserved for general-election subsidies. If additional funds are available, primary candidates may qualify for matching funds, which are distributed on a pro-rated basis.[113]

ELIGIBILITY AND CONDITIONS FOR PUBLIC FUNDING

Proponents of public financing generally argue that unlimited private funding encourages corruption, or at least forces candidates to spend too much time raising money. Therefore, states often require that recipients of public funding observe certain conditions on campaign conduct, which are designed to increase public confidence in campaigns and limit or eliminate large amounts of time spent raising private funds. Publicly financed candidates must agree to limits on spending and fundraising. Some states also require publicly financed candidates to participate in debates. Public funding recipients must demonstrate that they are politically viable by raising a minimum level of private contributions before becoming eligible for public funding. Some states' individual contributions are limited to as little as $5. Once candidates meet that threshold and other qualifying requirements, they become eligible for public financing. In most cases, campaigns qualifying for public financing may spend their privately raised contributions directly. In others, privately raised "seed money" is transferred to a central state fund for redistribution among all publicly financed candidates.

PARTICIPATION BY CANDIDATES

How widely candidates take advantage of public financing depends largely on whether opponents choose to participate in public financing, how various states structure their public financing programs, or both. Public financing programs often become dormant because potential participants believe that spending limits are too low. In Maryland, for example, although public financing is available for gubernatorial tickets, no major candidate has accepted that funding since 1994. Since that time, major candidates have reportedly viewed the 30-cent-per-voter spending limit as too low to enable effective campaigning.[114]

Low participation by candidates in public financing does not necessarily mean that the program fails to influence campaigns. At least one state's program appears to have the most impact when public financing is not utilized at all. Nebraska's public financing program has offered matching funds to a variety of statewide and legislative candidates since 1992, although it is rarely accepted. According to Frank Daley, Executive Director of the state's Accountability and Disclosure Commission, public financing in Nebraska becomes available only if one candidate adheres to spending limits while the other does not. If both candidates exceed spending limits, or if neither candidate exceeds spending limits, neither is eligible for public financing. Essentially, public financing in the state offers "extra" money for those facing high-spending opponents. Given the threat of opponents receiving public funds, most candidates have chosen to limit spending voluntarily. As a result, public financing's greatest impact in Nebraska appears to be keeping private spending down, rather than infusing greater amounts of public money into elections.[115]

Table 1. States Offering Public Financing to Statewide or Legislative Candidate Campaigns*

State	Candidates Eligible for Funding	How Candidates Receive Public Funding	How Public Financing System Is Funded	Notes
Arizona	Statewide (Governor, Lt. Governor, Secretary of State, Attorney General, Treasurer, Supt. of Public Instruction, Corporation Commissioner, Mine Inspector) State Legislature	Fixed subsidy Matching funds (contingency mechanism, e.g., for those facing non-publicly financed opponents who exceed spending limits)[b]	Tax checkoff Various fines/fees Qualifying private contributions raised by candidates	Clean money[a] model
Connecticut	Statewide (Governor, Lt. Governor, Attorney General, Comptroller, Secretary of State, Treasurer) State Legislature	Fixed subsidy Matching funds (contingency mechanism, e.g., for those facing non-publicly financed opponents who exceed spending limits)	Revenues from unclaimed property[c] Public donations	Clean money[a] model
Florida	Statewide (Governor, Chief Financial Officer, Attorney General, Agriculture Commissioner)[d]	Matching funds	Appropriations from legislature	See table notes.[d]

Table 1. Continued

State	Candidates Eligible for Funding	How Candidates Receive Public Funding	How Public Financing System Is Funded	Notes
Hawaii	Statewide (Governor, Lt. Governor, Office of Hawaiian Affairs) State Legislature	Matching funds	Tax checkoff Elections-related fines and fees Other miscellaneous fees[e]	
Maine	Statewide (Governor)[f] State Legislature	Fixed subsidy Matching funds (contingency mechanism, e.g., for those facing non-publicly financed opponents who exceed spending limits)	Tax checkoff Various fines/fees Appropriations from legislature Excess qualifying contributions raised by candidates	Clean money[a] model
Maryland	Statewide (Governor, Lt. Governor)	Matching funds	Tax checkoff[g]	No major candidate has participated since 1994, reportedly due to spending limits.

Table 1. Continued

State	Candidates Eligible for Funding	How Candidates Receive Public Funding	How Public Financing System Is Funded	Notes
Massachusetts	Statewide (Governor, Lt. Governor, Attorney General, Secretary of the Commonwealth, Treasurer, Auditor) State Legislature	Matching funds	Tax checkoff	Availability of public funding depends on the amount designated by tax checkoffs. Funding is allocated first to gubernatorial candidates, then lower offices, if available.[h]
Michigan	Statewide (Governor)[i]	Matching funds (primary election) Fixed subsidy (general election)	Tax checkoff	General election is funded first. Public financing for primary, if available, is then allocated on a pro-rated basis.[j]
Minnesota	Statewide (Governor, Lt. Governor, Attorney General, Secretary of State, Auditor)[k] State Legislature	Fixed subsidy	Tax checkoff Appropriations from legislature "Public Subsidy" funds[l]	

Table 1. Continued

State	Candidates Eligible for Funding	How Candidates Receive Public Funding	How Public Financing System Is Funded	Notes
Nebraska	Statewide (Governor, Secretary of State, Attorney General, Auditor of Public Accounts, Public Service Commission, Univ. of Nebraska Board of Regents, Board of Education) State Legislature	Matching funds	Tax checkoff Various fines/fees Initial appropriation from legislature[m]	
New Jersey	Statewide (Governor)	Matching funds	Appropriations from legislature Tax checkoff	
	State Legislature (pilot program)[n]	Direct subsidy	Appropriations from legislature	Clean money[a] model
New Mexico	Statewide (Public Regulation Commission; Judges for State Court of Appeals, State Supreme Court justices)	Fixed subsidy Matching funds (contingency mechanism, e.g., for those facing non-publicly financed opponents who exceed spending limits)	Appropriations from legislature Various fines/fees Unspent previous public financing monies[o]	Clean money[a] model

Table 1. Continued

State	Candidates Eligible for Funding	How Candidates Receive Public Funding	How Public Financing System Is Funded	Notes
North Carolina	Statewide (Judges for State Court of Appeals, State Supreme Court justices)	Fixed subsidy	Tax checkoff Attorney renewal fees	Public financing available only to judicial candidates. Clean money[a] model.[p]
Rhode Island	Statewide (Governor, Lt. Governor, Secretary of State, Attorney General, General Treasurer)	Matching funds	Tax checkoff Appropriations from legislature (secondary source)[q]	
Vermont	Statewide (Governor, Lt. Governor)	Fixed subsidy	Corporate reporting fees (primary source) Unspent previous public financing monies Tax checkoff Appropriations from legislature Public donations[r]	Clean money[a] model

Table 1. Continued

State	Candidates Eligible for Funding	How Candidates Receive Public Funding	How Public Financing System Is Funded	Notes
Wisconsin	Statewide (Governor, Lt. Governor, Attorney General, Secretary of State, Treasurer, Supt. of Public Instruction, State Supreme Court justices) State Legislature	Fixed subsidy	Tax checkoff	Availability of public funding depends on the amount designated by tax checkoffs.[s]

*Unless otherwise noted, all public financing programs reflected in the table apply to primary and general elections. The table does not include information on public funding for local candidates.

Source: CRS research as described in the text above and the following notes.

Notes:

a. The clean money model (often also called clean elections) offers full public financing to candidates who agree to certain restrictions, particularly spending limits. Public financing programs in Arizona and Maine are the most prominent statewide examples of this program, advocated by the interest group Public Campaign. Throughout the table, those programs noted as clean money reflect information on the Public Campaign website at [http://www.publicampaign.org/where], although this does not necessarily mean that there is a formal connection between Public Campaign and the public financing programs in those states.

b. This information came from Michael Becker, Voter Education Manager at the Citizens Clean Elections Commission (telephone conversation with R. Sam Garrett, Aug. 16, 2006).

c. According to Janice Thompson, a consultant for Public Campaign, if property proceeds do not meet public financing needs, the state may appropriate funds from corporate tax revenues to compensate for the shortfall (telephone conversation with R. Sam Garrett, Aug. 24, 2006). Thompson also provided CRS with additional summary information about Connecticut's public financing program.

d. The 2006 Center for Governmental Studies (CGS) report also refers to "qualifying candidates" for Lieutenant Governor and Corporations Commissioner as being eligible for public financing. See Steven M. Levin, *Keeping It Clean: Public Financing in American Elections*, p. 93. The CGS report also references various fines and fees to fund the state's Campaign Financing Trust fund. According to Kristi Reid Bronson, Election Records Bureau Chief at the Florida Division of Elections, the trust fund no longer exists, although it was funded by fines and fees. Bronson also reported that public financing — essentially funded by appropriations from the legislature — is available to the Governor and members of the cabinet (telephone conversation with R. Sam Garrett, Aug. 24, 2006). As of 2003, the Governor's cabinet includes the Attorney General, Chief Financial Officer, and Commissioner of Agriculture. For additional information, see "Cabinet Process Summary"; document posted on the Florida Department of State website at [http://www.myflorida.com/myflorida/cabinet/cabprocess.html].

e. According to public financing information on the Common Cause website at [http://www.commoncause.org/site/pp.asp?c=dkLNK1MQIwG&b=507399], Hawaii's program is also funded by appropriations. The 2006 Center for Governmental Studies report also refers to "appropriated funds" when summarizing Hawaii's public financing system. See Steven M. Levin, *Keeping It Clean: Public Financing in American Elections*, p. 93. Based on consultations with staff at Hawaii's Campaign Spending Commission, only those methods reflected in Table 1 currently fund the program (telephone conversation between R. Sam Garrett and a staff member, Hawaii Campaign Spending Commission, July 12, 2006). As the commission's *Public Funding Guidebook: Candidate Committees* explains, the legislature created the Hawaii Election Campaign Fund in 1979. See State of Hawaii, Campaign Spending Commission, *Public Funding Guidebook: Candidate Committees*, Jan. 2006, p. i, at [http://www.hawaii.gov/campaign/Forms/Publications/CCPublications/PFGuidebook/Public%20Funding%20Guidebook%20Candidate%20Committees.pdf]. This might explain other references to "appropriations."

f. According to Sandy Thompson, a candidate registrar at the Maine Commission on Governmental Ethics and Election Practices, the Governor is the only statewide elected officeholder (other than federal officeholders); telephone conversation with R. Sam Garrett, Aug. 17, 2006.

g. The 2006 Center for Governmental Studies (CGS) report also refers to direct appropriations and fines when summarizing Maryland's public financing system. See Steven M. Levin, *Keeping It Clean: Public Financing in American Elections*, p. 93. Jared DeMarinis, Maryland's director of candidacy and campaign finance, reported that a tax checkoff system financed the program when it was last utilized (telephone conversation with R. Sam Garrett, June 30, 2006). He also noted, however, that public financing legislation that failed in 2006 would have authorized additional funding sources and extended public financing to legislative candidates. According to DeMarinis, the same legislation, modeled on the Clean Money framework, is expected to be re-introduced during a future legislative session (telephone conversation with R. Sam Garrett, Aug. 24, 2006).

h. This information is based on consultations with staff at the Massachusetts Office of Campaign and Political Finance (telephone conversation with R. Sam Garrett, July 12, 2006). The 2006 CGS report also refers to direct appropriations and monies from a previous public financing fund when summarizing funding for Massachusetts's public financing system. See Steven M. Levin, *Keeping It Clean: Public Financing in American Elections*, p. 93. In 1998, Massachusetts voters, though a ballot initiative, approved a broad public financing program for the state. That program was based on the Clean Money model. However, the legislature did not appropriate funds for the program. The law was reportedly repealed in 2003, and replaced with the current system. See Thomas M. Finneran, "The Case Against Taxpayer Financing: A View From Massachusetts"; and the "Massachusetts" entry on the Common Cause website's description of state public-financing programs at [http://www.commoncause.org/site/pp.asp?c=dkLNK1MQIwG&b=507399].

i. The 2006 CGS report notes that public financing is available to candidates for Governor and Lieutenant Governor. See Steven M. Levin, *Keeping It Clean: Public Financing in American Elections*, p. 93. Based on consultations with staff at Michigan's Campaign Finance Division, public financing is only available for gubernatorial candidates (telephone conversation with R. Sam Garrett, Aug. 16, 2006). Information posted on the Common Cause website also suggests that funding is limited to gubernatorial candidates; see [http://www.commoncause.org/site/pp.asp?c=dkLNK1MQIwG&b=507399].

j. This information is based on consultations with staff at Michigan's Campaign Finance Division (telephone conversation with R. Sam Garrett, Aug. 2, 2006).

k. According to Jeanne Olson, Executive Director of the Minnesota Campaign Finance and Public Disclosure Board, the state's public financing system provides funding to the gubernatorial ticket, which would include the Lt. Governor candidate. The latter office, however, is not allocated separate public financing (telephone conversation with R. Sam Garrett, Aug. 18, 2006).

l. Public financing monies are distributed from the state's General Fund, as allocated through the tax check-off, and an additional appropriation from the state legislature. In addition, candidates agreeing to certain conditions (e.g., spending limits) may participate in the Public Subsidy program, which provides refunds from the state for private campaign contributions from individuals (telephone conversation between R. Sam Garrett and Jeanne Olson, Executive Director, Minnesota Campaign Finance and Public Disclosure Board, Aug. 18, 2006). For a brief overview of the Public Subsidy program, see "'Public Subsidy Issues," document posted on the Minnesota Campaign Finance and Public Disclosure Board website, Nov. 2005, at [http://www.cfboard.state.mn.us/issues/public_subsidy.pdf].

m. The 2006 CGS report refers to direct appropriations, taxpayer contributions of income tax refunds, "amounts repaid to campaign finance limitation cash fund by candidates," civil penalties, and late filing fees when summarizing how Nebraska's public financing system is funded. See Steven M. Levin, *Keeping It Clean: Public Financing in American Elections*, p. 94. Common Cause also lists "appropriations" as a funding source; see [http://www.commoncause.org/site/pp.asp?c=dkLNK1MQIwG&b=507399]. In a telephone consultation with one of the CRS authors, Frank Daley, Executive Director of the Nebraska Accountability and Disclosure Commission, reported that the legislature provided an initial appropriation of $50,000 in 1992, but has not done so since. Currently, according to Daley, the tax checkoff and various fines and fees are the only funding sources for public financing (telephone conversation with R. Sam Garrett, July 31, 2006).

n. During the 2005 election cycle, an experimental public financing program was implemented in two General Assembly districts. A May 2006 final report issued by the New Jersey Citizens' Clean Elections Commission recommended that the legislature continue the program for the 2007 cycle. In September 2007, Assembly Speaker Joseph J. Roberts, Jr., "Announced the creation of a ...working group charged with the mission of drafting legislation" to reauthorize public financing for a "limited number of legislative campaigns in 2007." See New Jersey Citizens' Clean Elections Commission, *Final Report*, submitted to the Legislature of the State of New Jersey, May 8, 2006, at [http://www.njleg.state.nj.us/committees/NJCCEC_FINAL.pdf]. For legislative background on the program and a brief historical overview, see New Jersey Citizens' Clean Elections Commission, *Preliminary Report*, submitted to Legislature of the State of New Jersey, Feb. 7, 2006: see [http://www.njleg.state.nj.us/committees/ PRELIM_REPORT_FINAL2.pdf]; and New Jersey General Assembly, "Roberts Announces Bipartisan Working Group to Reauthorize Clean Elections for 2007," press release, Sept. 7, 2006. A third legislative district was, according to a media account, added to the pilot project in April 2007. See Tom Hester, "14th District picked to join pilot program for 'clean elections,'' *Star-Ledger*; available at [http://www.nj.com/news/ledger/jersey/index.ssf?/base/news-6/117678616025121210.xml&coll=1]; accessed April 29, 2007. CRS confirmed the addition of the 14th district with staff at the New Jersey Citizens' Clean Elections Commission (telephone consultation with R. Sam Garrett, April 30, 2007).

o. Some of the summary information about New Mexico's public financing program came from the 2006 CGS report. See Steven M. Levin, *Keeping It Clean: Public Financing in American Elections*, p. 95. Clean Money programs generally rely on a grant system to distribute funding. Janice Thompson, a consultant for Public Campaign, reported that her research suggests that the New Mexico program is funded primarily by utility fees and taxes (telephone conversations with R. Sam Garrett, Aug. 2006), which is consistent with the CGS findings. The preceding applies to the Public Regulation Commission component of the program, which became effective for the 2006 election cycle. In April 2007, Governor Bill Richardson signed legislation extending public financing to elections for state appeals court judges and Supreme Court justices. See Gov. Bill Richardson, "Gov. Richardson Signs Landmark Public Financing Bill," press release; April 13, 2007; accessed April 27, 2007, by CRS Information Professional Zina Watkins via LexisNexis.

p. Some of the information about North Carolina's public financing program reflected in the table came from Jason Schrader, Audit Specialist in the Campaign Finance Division at the North Carolina Board of Elections (telephone conversations with R. Sam Garrett, Aug. 2006). For an early assessment of North Carolina's first cycle of public financing for judicial candidates, see Doug Bend, "North Carolina's Public Financing of Judicial Campaigns: A Preliminary Analysis," *The Georgetown Journal of Legal Ethics*, vol. 18, no. 3 (summer 2005), pp. 597-609.

q. The 2006 CGS report lists only a checkoff as the funding mechanism for Rhode Island's public financing system. See Steven M. Levin, *Keeping It Clean: Public Financing in American Elections*, p. 97. Rhode Island law authorizes the state treasury to provide monies from the state's general fund if "funds generated by the tax credit…fail to produce sufficient money to meet the requirements of the public financing of the electoral system." See R.I. G.L. § 17-25-29 at [http://www.rilin.state.ri.us/Statutes/TITLE17/ 17-25/17-25-29.HTM]. "Tax credit" in the preceding sentence appears to be a reference to the tax checkoff system. Hank Johnson, a staff member in the Campaign Finance Division at the Rhode Island Board of Elections, confirmed that the program is financed by the checkoff system and general fund revenues distributed by the state treasury (telephone conversation with R. Sam Garrett, August 2006).

r. According to information from staff at the Vermont Secretary of State's office, corporate reporting fees are the major source of funding for the state's public financing program, and that not all other sources of funding authorized by statute have been utilized (telephone conversation with R. Sam Garrett, Aug. 2006).

s. Some of this information came from Dennis Morvak, an auditor in the Campaign Finance Division at the Wisconsin Elections Board (telephone conversations with R. Sam Garrett, Aug. 22, 2006). Common Cause reports that "In recent years, the system has been damaged by a decline in the amount of funds generated by the check-off and growing spending on independent expenditures and sham 'issue ads.'" This report takes no position on Common Cause's statement regarding issue advertising. The text of this report provides additional information on the Wisconsin program, including citations to other critiques.

IMPACT OF PUBLIC FINANCING IN THE STATES

Despite recent scholarly research, there is little certainty about how changes in American campaign finance law affect electoral outcomes.[116] Research on the impact of public financing is particularly limited, dated, or both. Public financing programs in the states vary widely and were implemented at different times. Even basic terminology can vary across states. All these factors limit opportunities for comparing data.[117] In answering whether public financing has achieved the various goals proponents ascribe, one group of scholars wrote in 2006:

> The short answer is that nobody knows because there has been no comprehensive evaluation of public finance systems to identify what conditions and program elements lead to successful outcomes. The conventional wisdom is based on either a limited amount of data or anecdotal impression.[118]

Similarly, much of what is known about public financing is based on relatively narrow evaluations of particular states or races.

Money and Competition

One of the major questions surrounding public financing is whether publicly funded campaigns are more or less competitive than those that are privately financed. Research often considers at least two different measures of "competition" surrounding public financing: (1) the amount of money at each campaign's disposal; and (2) the margin of victory on election day. In theory, public financing should foster lower-cost campaigns because public financing generally requires observing spending limits and reduces fundraising costs. If more candidates have access to funding through public financing, races might also be closer on election day.[119] Evidence on both fronts is mixed. In general, research suggests that public financing can foster more competitive elections. However, research on competition and public financing commonly emphasizes that most public financing programs are in their infancy, and that more time and cases are needed to draw definitive conclusions.

Public financing does appear to reduce financial disparities among candidates, provided that all candidates participate in public financing. For example, research on state legislative elections has found that public financing in Minnesota and Wisconsin decreased financial disparities between challengers and incumbents.[120] More access to money via public funding does not always foster closer races,[121] although it can provide ballot access for candidates who might not otherwise be able to run.[122] From this perspective, public financing provides an avenue to consistent competition in elections, but not necessarily closer elections. On the other hand, in a comparative analysis of legislative elections in five states that offer public financing — Arizona, Hawaii, Maine, Minnesota, and Wisconsin — political scientists Kenneth R. Mayer, Timothy Werner, and Amanda Williams found that competition generally increased after public financing was enacted, both in terms of the number of incumbents facing challengers, and the number of "competitive" races.[123] These findings, however, were contingent upon sufficient funding to make the programs attractive to candidates. Finally, there is some anecdotal evidence of public financing favoring challengers or Democrats, although these findings are not systematic, and other research disputes such findings.[124]

Regardless of candidates eligible for funding or the particulars of individual campaigns, public financing becomes less popular, and therefore has less impact, if not all major candidates have incentives to participate. Recent experience with Wisconsin's program, for example, suggests that publicly financed elections in that state have not become more competitive. Some observers suggest that Wisconsin's program provides too little funding to be a major component of candidate's overall expenditures. Hawaii has reportedly experienced similar problems.[125]

Time Spent Fundraising

Some who support public financing suggest that it can lead to more substantive campaigns by freeing candidates from the burdens of raising large private contributions, providing more time to connect with voters and discuss policy issues.[126] Research indicates that public financing does decrease the amount of time state legislative candidates spend raising money, but the finding holds only for full public financing. A national survey of candidates who ran for state legislatures in 2000 revealed that "[f]ull public funding can free candidates from spending large amounts of time 'dialing for dollars' or making personal appeals to prospective donors. By comparison, candidates who accepted partial public funds devoted about the same time to fundraising as did candidates in states that did not provide public funding."[127] If this finding holds in other kinds of races, it suggests that *partial* public financing might do little to alleviate what has been called "the money chase" of continual fundraising.[128] By contrast, existing models of *full* public financing can reduce candidates' fundraising duties for individual campaigns. Nonetheless, despite the assertion that full public funding "can free candidates to spend less time with wealthy donors raising money and more time on other aspects of campaigning,"[129] it is unclear whether public financing makes campaigns more "substantive," or how such concepts would be measured. In addition, public financing would not necessarily free candidates from fundraising for leadership PACs or other entities that may serve to benefit their elections indirectly.[130]

Diversity Among Candidates and Donors

Those favoring public financing suggest that it democratizes campaigns by providing more "average" people with the resources to run, and enhances the role of small donations from ordinary citizens. There is some evidence that public financing allows candidates who would not otherwise do so, including minorities and women, to run for office.[131] Clean Money programs requiring candidates to collect small private contributions (e.g., $5 in Maine) also potentially expand the donor universe by creating an important financial role for ordinary citizens who might be unable to make large private contributions.[132]

The Impact of Recent Public Financing Efforts in Arizona and Maine

Much of the recent attention to public financing has occurred because of notable ballot initiatives in two states. In 1996 and 1998, respectively, Maine and Arizona became the first states to provide full public financing for qualified candidates for statewide and legislative offices. These two states are often considered test cases for public financing because their programs are so comprehensive. In both states, the first disbursements under these programs were made in the 2000 election cycle.[133] Both states adopted public financing modeled on the clean money program, advocated by Public Campaign. Arizona and Maine offer similar full public financing to statewide and legislative candidates. Although Connecticut also recently adopted similar public financing, the program has not yet been fully implemented.

BCRA[134] directed the General Accounting Office (GAO, now the Government Accountability Office) to study Arizona and Maine's public financing programs. The GAO report, issued in May 2003 and based on public financing offered in the 2000 and 2002 election cycles, found "inconclusive" and "mixed" results.[135] According to GAO, "In sum, with only two elections from which to observe legislative races and only one election from which to observe most statewide races, it is too early to draw causal linkages to changes, if any, that resulted from the public financing programs in the two states."[136] GAO also found "inconclusive" and "mixed" results when examining whether the states met program goals in five areas: (1) voter choice (measured in candidate emergence and participation in public financing); (2) electoral competition (measured in percentage of competitive elections, decreases in incumbent reelection rates, or smaller victory margins for reelected incumbents); (3) interest group influence (measured by candidate and interest group reports through interviews and surveys); (4) campaign spending (measured in candidate spending and independent expenditures); and (5) voter participation (measured in turnout and awareness in surveys of public financing).[137] GAO found that despite program goals of increasing the number of candidates running for office and making elections more competitive, "the average numbers of state legislature candidates per district race in Maine or Arizona in the 2000 and 2002 elections were not notably different than the averages for the two previous elections, 1996 and 1998" (which did not have public financing). GAO also found "inconclusive" results with respect to changes in competition in the two states under public financing.[138] Another group of researchers, however, found that the number of contested races in Arizona legislative elections increased by more than 10% from 2002 to 2004.[139] There is also anecdotal evidence of increased competition in districts that would have been uncompetitive under private campaign financing, although at least one analysis suggests that Maine's program has not fostered more competitive elections.[140]

Despite contradictory data on effectiveness, candidate participation in both states' public financing programs "increased greatly" between 2000 and 2002.[141] In 2004, majorities of candidates in both states participated in public financing. In Arizona, 25% of candidates participated in public financing in the 2000 primary election, compared with 27% in the general election. In 2002, those numbers increased to 52% and 50%, respectively.[142] In 2004, 61% of primary candidates (statewide and legislative) participated in the clean money system, compared with 56% of general-election candidates.[143] By contrast, in Maine, about one-third of candidates participated in public financing during the 2000 primary and general elections. By 2002, 51% of candidates participated in public financing during the primary, and 62% participated during the general election.[144] In 2004, 78% of general-election candidates for the Maine legislature participated in public financing.[145] In the 2006 primary, 77% of Maine legislative candidates participated in public financing, as did 80% during the general election.[146] In 2004 and 2006, more Maine Democrats than Republicans participated, but large majorities of members of both parties did so.[147] Preliminary data for 2006 indicated that approximately 61% of primary candidates in Arizona participated in public financing, as did approximately 60% of general election candidates. (These figures represent candidates for all offices, not only legislative candidates).[148]

Candidates reported in surveys that they chose to accept public funding because they did not want to feel beholden to private financiers, and believed that accepting public funding allowed them to spend more campaign time "discussing issues."[149] Conversely, candidates in both states cited a variety of reasons for choosing *not* to participate in public financing, including ideological opposition to public funding, a belief that they could win without public funds, and an unwillingness to restrict campaign spending as required for receiving public funds.[150]

Some observers have questioned the Arizona and Maine programs on ideological or legal grounds.[151] Fundamental to those arguments is that citizens could be indirectly forced to provide financial support to politicians with whom they disagree, since Arizona's program is financed through various fines and fees.[152] Some critics of Arizona's program also contend that increased competition in the state's elections could be due to other factors, such as the impact of term limits.[153] In addition, Maine's program is, according to one report favoring public financing, "plagued by private contributions to candidate leadership PACs."[154] One report also found that although Maine's program reduced "the role of private money in election campaigns," and although publicly financed challengers were able to attain "financial parity" with incumbents, the long-term impact on electoral competition was unclear.[155] Political scientists Ray La Raja and Matthew Saradjian have raised the possibility that public financing could increase independent expenditures by interest groups and other organizations.[156]

PUBLIC OPINION ON PUBLIC FINANCING AND SPENDING LIMITS

Surveys indicate that Americans generally support campaign finance "reform" (generally meaning more regulation of money in politics) and are concerned about the amount of money in campaigns. Nonetheless, public opinion about campaign finance can be contradictory.[157] These patterns are evident in the relatively limited available data about attitudes on public financing. Historically, surveys reveal that large pluralities or even majorities of Americans support public financing in principle, but are hesitant to invest tax dollars to facilitate public financing. These findings indicate that the wording, source, and timing of individual questions vary greatly and can affect campaign finance polling results, as is always the case with survey research, regardless of topic.

Majorities tend to support public financing when asked questions suggesting favorable information about public financing, or in surveys conducted for pro-reform clients.[158] On the other hand, majorities tend to respond negatively to questions focusing on costs of public financing or taxation.[159] Survey respondents say that they are neutral or positive toward public financing if question wording suggests that public financing can limit the influence of "special interests" or campaign costs.[160] On the other hand, survey questions that emphasize spending "taxpayer dollars" to support public financing often yield disapproval from respondents. Americans have been more willing in polls to support public financing after perceived scandals, such as during the 1970s and 1990s.[161]

In Gallup polling conducted between 1972 and 1996, between 50% and 65% of respondents favored "provid[ing] a fixed amount of money" for presidential and congressional campaigns, while banning private contributions.[162] Similarly, in a 1997 *Washington Post* poll, 49% of campaign contributors answered favorably when asked if they would "favor or oppose having all federal elections financed out of public funds, with strict limits on how much each candidate for president, US Senator or Congressman could spend"; 48% were opposed.[163] In the same poll, but with spending limits omitted from question wording, only 26% responded favorably when asked whether they would "favor or oppose the federal government financing presidential and congressional elections out of tax money."[164]

The polling data reviewed above illustrate that Americans have more consistently supported containing campaign spending — a hallmark of public financing programs — than public funding per se. For example, in a 1997 *New York Times*/CBS News poll, 60% of respondents said that "limit[ing] the amount of money that campaigns can spend" should be a "top" or "high" priority within campaign finance reform efforts.[165] In a Gallup poll from the same year, 79% of respondents favored "putting a limit on the amount of money" congressional candidates could "raise and spend on their political campaigns."[166] However, like all survey questions, answers to spending questions are also affected by wording. For example, in a 1999 NBC News poll, only 17% of respondents (but the second-most-common answer) presented with a list of potential campaign finance concerns said that "unlimited contributions" concerned them most, compared with 37% who were most concerned about "special interests."[167] More generally, in a 2002 ABC News/*Washington Post* poll, 66% of respondents favored "stricter laws controlling the way political campaigns raise and spend money."[168] It appears that regular, national polling about public financing has been uncommon since the mid-1990s.

POTENTIAL CONSIDERATIONS FOR CONGRESSIONAL PUBLIC FINANCING

Public financing has been debated in Congress and the states for decades. This suggests that interest in the topic will continue. As Congress considers how, or whether, to change the status quo, state experiences with public financing, as well as the nation's presidential public financing system, offer several potential lessons. However, the great diversity among state programs makes interpreting those lessons challenging. At the federal level, the presidential public financing system provides partial matching funds to qualifying candidates in primaries, but far more substantial fixed subsidies to candidates in the general election. At the state level, which campaigns are eligible for public funding, how much funding is available, what requirements are placed on candidates accepting public funding, and when programs were implemented vary. The presidential public financing system and those in the states all rely on either fixed subsidies (in the states, especially clean money models) or matching funds to distribute public financing. Despite similar ways of delivering funds to candidates, details about each program can vary greatly. These differences have produced research that describes individual components of public financing programs, but rarely draws systematic comparisons across states. In addition, only two states — Arizona and Maine — currently provide full public financing for legislative elections. (Others provide partial public financing for legislative elections, but, again, vary widely.) Consequently, there are few certainties about how public financing might apply to congressional campaigns. Nonetheless, several potential considerations remain.

State models suggest two approaches[169] to national public financing if Congress decides to pursue subsidized congressional campaigns. First, most public financing programs infuse public money into campaigns in hopes of limiting the impact of private money. This approach essentially provides candidates with money so that they do not have to raise their own — or can at least raise less. Second, some models, such as Nebraska's public funding program, have reportedly encouraged the vast majority of candidates to limit spending on their own. Rather than providing public funding to candidates based on the assumption that they will spend those funds, the Nebraska program reserves public financing for candidates whose opponents refuse to abide by relatively low spending limits. These two approaches suggest a choice for Congress between public funding that concentrates primarily on distributing money in anticipation of campaign needs versus creating incentives for candidates to need less money by observing spending limits.[170]

In addition, creating a public financing system requires a choice between funding primary elections or general elections, or both. Most existing state programs have funded both types of elections, although general elections sometimes take priority over primary elections and might be funded differently from primary elections. While early congressional proposals generally covered primaries as well as general elections, most prominent proposals since the 100th Congress have dealt only with general election financing to reduce both costs and program complexity, and to enhance chances for enactment.

Regardless of the chosen approach, public financing does not altogether eliminate private money in politics. Even clean money programs require some private fundraising to establish viability, albeit far less than under private financing. In addition, some observers fear that public financing creates opportunities for more financial influence from less accountable non-candidate sources — such as independent expenditures and election-related "issue advocacy" by interest groups — compared with the current system of private financing. Public financing systems generally do not regulate fundraising or spending outside candidate campaigns, although legislation could address such issues.

Congress might also wish to consider why some public financing programs have been curtailed. In a few states, decisions by voters and candidates — not state governments — appear to be most responsible for public financing programs falling into disfavor. Experiences in the states suggest that in order to be viable, public financing must have sufficient funding to make participation attractive to candidates. As with public funds for presidential candidates, if public financing provides too little money — or sets accompanying spending limits too low — to convince candidates that they can wage effective campaigns, major candidates are likely to opt out of the system, ultimately making it relevant only for minor candidates. (In 2004, for example, both of the eventual major-party nominees for President opted out of matching funds in the primaries.) Public support can also be important to enact and maintain public financing. Despite regular congressional interest in public financing since at least the 1950s, disagreements over many of the issues noted in this report have thus far thwarted efforts to adopt public financing in legislative elections.

On a related note, effective public financing[171] requires resources not only adequate to make participation attractive to candidates, but also sufficient to administer and enforce public financing. As law professor Richard Briffault has explained,

> Public [campaign] funding requires administrators to determine who qualifies for public funds, to disburse the funds, and to enforce whatever restrictions accompany the funds. Can public administrators handle the job? In fact, administrators have successfully handled the qualification of candidates and disbursement of public funds in presidential elections. The real question is whether they can enforce the rules — particularly the spending limits — that are likely to accompany public funding.[172]

Comprehensive congressional public financing would, therefore, almost certainly require substantial administrative and enforcement resources for the Federal Election Commission.

Finally, public financing regulates only one area of campaign conduct. If Congress were to adopt public financing for its elections, other regulations —including those currently in place — would still be required to shape other areas of campaign politics, such as political advertising and party activities. Public financing would also not necessarily affect other factors that shape individual races. As one pair of scholars wrote in 1995,

> public financing of congressional elections, by itself, will not eliminate the problem of uncompetitive elections. As in Wisconsin, public subsidies may increase or prevent further deterioration in the competitiveness of contested congressional races by giving challengers more of a level playing field. They might not, however, encourage challengers to emerge in districts where the incumbent is perceived as unbeatable.[173]

Public financing could have diverse impacts on congressional elections. Data from the states show some evidence that public financing decreases financial disparities between candidates and fosters closer margins of victory. However, these findings are generally preliminary and are based on specific conditions in specific states. Because public financing limits the amount of private financing of campaigns, it is likely that public financing in congressional elections would reduce the amount of time candidates spend raising money — at least for their own or others' candidate campaigns. On its own, however, public financing of candidate campaigns would not affect activities by 527s, political parties, or other organizations. The same is true for leadership PACs, unless they were prohibited by public financing legislation.

Evidence from the states also suggests that if Congress chooses to fund congressional elections publicly, faith in the system and patience will be required. As is discussed throughout this report, much about the impact of public financing is simply unknown. Relatively few states offer public financing for legislative elections. Individual components of those programs, such as funding levels, conditions on candidates, and other factors, can vary substantially, making it difficult to compare public financing across states or to draw firm inferences about how state lessons might translate to congressional elections. It is clear from the presidential public financing program, and state programs, that assessing the impact of public financing takes multiple election cycles. As more states experiment with legislative public financing, and do so for longer periods of time, potential lessons for adopting congressional public financing will become clearer. It is also clear that in order to be effective, public financing programs require levels of funding sufficient to make them attractive to serious candidates, and to maintain those levels of funding over time. Similarly, spending limits associated with public financing must be high enough to convince candidates that they can compete in modern campaigns, including in expensive broadcast media markets.

APPENDIX 1.
PUBLIC FINANCE BILLS PASSED BY THE HOUSE OR SENATE: 1973 – 1993[174]

Table 2. Congressional Election Public Finance Bills Passed by House or Senate: Summary of Provisions

Congress, Bill, & Action	Applicability		Public Benefits		Spending Limits	Notes
	Chamber	Election	Direct Payments	Other Benefits		
93rd Congress H.R. 11104, S. Amt. 651 Passed by Senate Nov. 27, 1973	House	General	Major-party candidates: Fixed subsidy equal to spending limit Minor-party candidates: Fixed subsidy based on prior vote history		Greater of 15¢ per eligible voter, or $90,000 Parties may spend additional amounts	Mandatory system Financed by negative tax checkoff (i.e., one must opt not to have tax revenues used)
Later dropped after House refused to accept Senate additions	Senate	General	Major-party candidates: Fixed subsidy equal to spending limit Minor-party candidates: Fixed subsidy based on prior vote history		Greater of 15¢ per eligible voter, or $175,000 Parties may spend additional amounts	

Table 2. Continued

Congress, Bill, & Action	Applicability Chamber	Applicability Election	Public Benefits Direct Payments	Public Benefits Other Benefits	Spending Limits	Notes
93rd Cong. S. 3044 Passed by Senate Apr. 11, 1974	House	Primary	Matches $100 donations, up to ½ spending limit		$90,000	Voluntary system
		General	Major-party candidates: Fixed subsidy equal to spending limit Minor party candidates: Fixed subsidy based on prior vote history		$90,000 Parties may spend additional amounts	Financed by negative tax checkoff (i.e., one must opt not to have tax revenues used)
	Senate	Primary	Matches $100 donations, up to ½ spending limit		Greater of 10¢ per eligible voter, or $125,000	
		General	Major-party candidates: Fixed subsidy equal to spending limit Minor party candidates: Fixed subsidy based on prior vote history		Greater of 15¢ per eligible voter, or $175,000 Parties may spend additional amounts	

Table 2. Continued

Congress, Bill, & Action	Applicability		Public Benefits			Spending Limits	Notes
	Chamber	Election	Direct Payments	Other Benefits			
101st Cong. S. 137 Passed Senate Aug. 1, 1990	Senate	General	— *Contingent subsidies to compensate participant for:* *(A) independent expenditures against participant or for opponent; and* *(B) expenditures by opponent in excess of spending limit*	Broadcast communication vouchers of up to 20% of general election spending limit Lowest unit rate for non-pre-emptible broadcast time Reduced mail rates, valued up to 5% of the general election limit (First-class mail at 1/4 existing rate; third-class mail at 2¢ less than existing rate)		Contributions or loans from candidate or family: $250,000 General election — The lesser of: (A) $5.5 million, or (B) the greater of (i) $950,000, or (ii) $400,000, plus 30¢ times the voting age population (VAP), up to 4 million, and 25¢ times VAP over 4 million (may be exceeded by 25%, in small in-state donations) Primary election — 67% of the general election limit, up to $2.75 million Runoff — 20% of the general election limit *Limits raised to equal independent expenditures against participants in primary and removed if opponent spends more than 133 1/3% of limit*	Candidates who do not participate are ineligible for lowest unit rate and are required to include in their advertisements a statement that they do not abide by spending limits Total spending range: $1.6 - $8.3 million

Table 2. Continued

Congress, Bill, & Action	Applicability		Public Benefits		Spending Limits	Notes
	Chamber	Election	Direct Payments	Other Benefits		

101st Congress H.R. 5400
 	
Passed House Aug. 3, 1990
	House	General	—	One free radio or TV spot for every two purchased
				
				First-class postage at ½ current rate and third-class postage at nonprofit rate, in the last 90 days of the election campaign
				
				100% tax credit for in-state contributors, up to $50 ($100 on joint returns)
					Candidate personal funds — $75,000
					
					Election cycle —
					   $550,000 (up to $300,000 in primary), plus:
					   $165,000 if primary is won with less than 2/3 of vote
					
					Runoff —
					   $100,000
					
					Contingency provision: Limits removed if non-participant raises or spends more than $200,000	

Table 2. Continued

Congress, Bill, & Action	Applicability		Public Benefits		Spending Limits	Notes
	Chamber	Election	Direct Payments	Other Benefits		

102nd Cong. S. 3
 	
Passed Senate May 23, 1991
	Senate	General	—
			
			Contingent subsidies to compensate participant for:
			(A) independent expenditures against participant or for opponent, once over $10,000; and
			(B) expenditures by opponent in excess of spending limit
				Broadcast communication vouchers of up to 20% of general election spending limit
				
				50% lowest unit rate for non-pre-emptible broadcast time
				
				Reduced mail rates, valued up to 5% of general election limit (first-class mail at 1/4 existing rate; third-class mail at 2¢ less than reduced first-class rate)
					Contributions or loans from candidate or family: $25,000
					
					General election —
					The lesser of:
					  (A) $5.5 million, or
					  (B) the greater of
					    (i) $950,000, or
					    (ii) $400,000, plus 30¢ times VAP, up to 4 million, and 25¢ times VAP over 4 million
					
					Primary election — 67% of general election limit, up to $2.75 million
					
					Runoff — 20% of general election limit
					
					Contingency provision: Limits raised to equal independent expenditures against participants in primary or general, once over $10,000, and removed if opponent spends more than 133 1/3% of limit
						Candidates who do not participate are required to include in their advertisements a statement that they do not abide by spending limits.
						
						(Total spending range: $1.6 million to $8.3 million)

Table 2. Continued

Congress, Bill, & Action	Applicability		Public Benefits		Spending Limits	Notes
	Chamber	Election	Direct Payments	Other Benefits		
102nd Congress H.R. 3750 Passed House Nov. 25, 1991	House	General	Matching funds, up to $200,000, with first $200 from individuals matched *Contingent subsidies to compensate participant:* *(A) for independent expenditures against participant or for opponent;* *(B) for expenditures by opponent once in excess of 50% of general election spending limit, on a matching basis; and* *(C) if opponent makes personal contributions in excess of 50% of general election limit, on 3- to-1 matching basis*	Up to three mailings per eligible voter, at same reduced third-class postage rate as available to national parties	Candidate personal funds — $60,000 Election cycle — $600,000 (up to $500,000 in general election), plus $150,000 if primary is won by 10% or less of vote Runoff — $100,000 *Contingency provision: Limits are removed if opponent raises or spends more than 50% of general election limit or when $60,000 in independent expenditures are made against the candidate or for opponent*	

Table 2. Continued

Congress, Bill, & Action	Applicability		Public Benefits		Spending Limits	Notes
	Chamber	Election	Direct Payments	Other Benefits		
102nd Congress S. 3 Conference version Vetoed May 9, 1992	Senate	General	— *Contingent subsidies to compensate participant for:* *(A) independent expenditures against participant or for opponent; and* *(B) expenditures by opponent in excess of spending limit*	Broadcast communication vouchers of up to 20% of gen. election spending limit 50% lowest unit rate for non-pre-emptible broadcast time Up to 1 mailing per eligible voter, at lowest 3rd class non-profit rate	Candidate/family contributions/ loans —lesser of $250,000, or 10% of general election limit General election — the lesser of: (A) $5.5 million, or (B) the greater of (i) $950,000, or (ii) $400,000, plus 30¢ times VAP, up to $4 million, and 25¢ times VAP over $4 million Primary election — 67% of general election limit, up to $2.75 million Runoff — 20% of general election limit *Contingency provision: Limits raised to equal independent expenditures against participants in general election, once over $10,000, and raised if opponent spends more than 133 1/3% of limit*	Non-participants required to run disclaimer on ads that they do not abide by spending limits (Total spending range: $1.6 million to $8.3 million)

Table 2. Continued

Congress, Bill, & Action	Applicability		Public Benefits		Spending Limits	Notes
	Chamber	Election	Direct Payments	Other Benefits		
102nd Congress S. 3 Conference version Vetoed May 9, 1992	House	General	Matching funds, up to $200,000, with first $200 from individuals matched *Contingent subsidies to compensate participant:* *(A) for independent expenditures against participant or for opponent, once over $10,000; and* *(B) if opponent makes personal contributions in excess of 50% of general election limit, on a 3- to-1 matching basis*	Up to 1 mailing per eligible voter, at lowest third-class, non-profit rate	Candidate personal funds — lesser of $250,000, or 10% of general election limit Election cycle — $600,000 (up to $500,000 in general election), plus: $150,000 if contested primary is won by 10% or less of vote Runoff — $100,000 *Contingency provision: Limits removed if opponent spends more than 80% of general election limit or to extent of independent expenditures made against candidate or opponent, once over $10,000*	

Table 2. Continued

Congress, Bill, & Action	Applicability		Public Benefits		Spending Limits	Notes
	Chamber	Election	Direct Payments	Other Benefits		
103rd Congress S. 3 Passed Senate June 17, 1993	Senate	General	— *Contingent subsidies to compensate participant for:* *(A) independent expenditures against participant or for opponent, once over $10,000 from a single source; and* *(B) expenditures by opponent in excess of spending limit*	50% lowest unit rate for non-pre-emptible broadcast time, in last 60 days of general election Up to 2 mailings per eligible voter, at lowest third-class, non-profit rate	Candidate/family contributions/loans — $25,000 General election — the lesser of: (A) $5.5 million, or (B) the greater of (i) $950,000, or (ii) $400,000, plus 30¢ times VAP, up to 4 million, and 25¢ times VAP over 4 million Primary election — 67% of general limit, up to $2.75 million Runoff — 20% of general limit *Contingency provision: Limits are raised to equal independent expenditures against participants in general election, once over $10,000, and raised if opponent exceeds limit by 100% of limit (but spending not to exceed 200% of limit)*	Non-participants required to run disclaimer on ads that they do not abide by spending limits Repeals exempt function income exclusion on principal campaign committees of candidates who exceed spending limits (Total spending range: $1.6 million to $8.9 million)

Table 2. Continued

Congress, Bill, & Action	Applicability		Public Benefits		Spending Limits	Notes
	Chamber	Election	Direct Payments	Other Benefits		
103rd Congress H.R. 3 Passed House Nov. 22, 1993	House	General	*Contingent subsidies to compensate participant for:* *(A) independent expenditures against participant or for opponent, once over $10,000; and* *(B) close-primary winners (up to $66,600 in additional vouchers)*	Voter communication vouchers, based on matching first $200 from individuals, up to $200,000	Candidate personal funds — $50,000 Election cycle — $600,000, plus: $200,000 if contested primary is won by 20% or less of vote Runoff — $200,000 *Contingency provision: Limits removed if non-participating opponent raises or spends more than 25% of general election limit or to extent of independent expenditures made against candidate or for opponent, once over $10,000*	

Note:
VAP = voting age population

APPENDIX 2.
PUBLIC FINANCE BILLS IN THE 109TH CONGRESS: SUMMARY OF KEY PROVISIONS

H.R. 2753 (Andrews) — Public Campaign Financing Act of 2005

(Introduced June 7, 2005; referred to Committee on House Administration)

Public Finance Provisions

- Would have provided public funding in House general elections in amounts based on media costs in the area, up to $750,000 (with indexing for future inflation), for specified campaign purposes (but not a salary for candidate), within four months of general election, for candidates who: (a) gather petitions signed by at least 3% of registered voters or whose party received at least 25% of the vote in prior general election; (b) limit individual donations to $100; (c) raise at least 80% of funds in-state; and (d) participate in at least two debates; would have required broadcasters to accept participating candidate ads, until they constituted 40% of station's total advertising time.

Other Provisions

- Would have required FEC to allow state parties to file copies of reports filed under state law if they contain substantially the same information as required under federal law;
- Would have required prompt disclosure by non-party entities for spending on "federal election activities" (as defined by BCRA), once $2,000 threshold level is reached;
- Would have required candidate reports to be broken down by primary, general, or runoff election;
- Would have prohibited bundling by PACs, parties, lobbyists, unions, corporations, or national banks, or employees or agents acting on their behalf.

H.R. 3099 (Tierney) — Clean Money, Clean Elections Act

(Introduced June 28, 2005; jointly referred to Committees on House Administration, Energy and Commerce, and Government Reform)

Public Finance Provisions

- Would have applied to House candidates voluntarily participating in public financing;
- Would have provided full public subsidies, 30 minutes of free broadcast time in primary and 75 minutes in general election, and additional broadcast time at 50% of lowest unit rate for House candidates who participate in "clean money" system and spend no private funds beyond subsidy once qualified;
- Would have allowed candidates, prior to qualification, to raise *seed money* ($35,000, in contributions of $100 or less) for specified uses by raising $5 donations from 1,500 state residents; others would have qualified by raising 150% of amount raised by major party candidates;
- Subsidy would have equaled applicable percentage (60% for general election, 40% for major party candidate in primary, and 25% for other primary candidates) of 80% of base amount per election (base amount would have been national average of winning House candidate expenditures in three most recent general

elections), but amount was never to be less than amount provided in previous election cycle;

- Would have reduced subsidy to 40% of amount otherwise determined for unopposed candidates;
- Additional subsidies would have been provided to candidates targeted in opposing independent expenditures and by noncomplying opponents once such spending exceeded 125% of spending limit (maximum additional funds equals 200% of limit);
- Would have denied lowest unit rate to non-participating House candidates;
- Would have financed benefits from House of Representatives Election Fund using appropriated funds, qualifying contributions, and unused seed money.

Other Provisions

- In House races with at least one "clean money" candidate, would have limited party spending on behalf of a candidate to 10% of general election candidate's subsidy;
- Regarding "clean money" candidates: would have required 48-hour notice of independent expenditures above $1,000 up to 20 days before election and 24-hour notice of amounts above $500 in last 20 days;
- Would have amended "contribution" to include anything of value for purpose of influencing a federal election and that was coordinated with candidate;
- Would have defined "payment made in coordination with a candidate" to include payments (1) in cooperation or consultation with, or at request or suggestion of, a candidate or agent; (2) using candidate-prepared materials; (3) based on information about campaign plans provided by candidate's campaign for purpose of expenditure; (4) by a spender who during that election cycle had acted in an official position for a candidate, in an executive, policymaking, or advisory capacity; and (5) by a spender who had used the same consultants as an affected candidate during election cycle; would have deemed payments made in coordination with a candidate as a "contribution" or "expenditure" (but exempted a payment by a party in coordination with a "clean money" candidate);

- Would have added one FEC commissioner, recommended by other members;
- Would have allowed random audits of campaigns;
- Would have given FEC authority to seek injunctions;
- Would have changed standard to begin enforcement proceedings to "reason to investigate";
- Would have allowed FEC to petition Supreme Court;
- !Would have expedited enforcement in last 60 days of election, with clear and convincing evidence that violation had occurred, was occurring, or was about to occur;
- Would have allowed subpoenas without chair's signature;
- Would have required electronic filing of disclosure reports;
- Would have required 24-hour notice of all contributions received in last 90 days of election;
- Would have prohibited preemption of House campaign broadcast ads, unless beyond broadcasters' control;
- Would have prohibited franked mass mailings from start of primary election period through general election, unless Member was not a candidate or mailing promotes public forum with candidate name only;
- Included statement of findings and declarations;
- If any provision of act or this statute were held unconstitutional, the remainder of act and statute would have been unaffected.

H.R. 4694 (Obey) — Let the Public Decide Campaign Finance Reform Act

(Introduced February 1, 2006; jointly referred to Committees on House Administration, Ways and Means, and Rules)

Public Finance Provisions

- Would have set mandatory limits on House general election spending based on median household income per district, with maximum of $1.5 million for all major party candidates in highest level district;
- Other districts' limits would have been determined by subtracting from $1.5 million: two-thirds of percentage difference between the

median household income in the district involved and the highest-median-household-income district, multiplied by $1.5 million;

- Maximum expenditure by a major party candidate would have been in the same ratio to the district-wide limit as the votes for that candidate's party in the last two House general elections in the district were to the votes for all major party candidates in those two elections;

- For purposes of establishing major party limit, only elections in which there were at least two major party candidates were to have been counted, and, if no such elections occurred, votes for Senate elections during the same period were to be used as the basis;

- Maximum expenditure for minor party or independent candidates would have been based on comparable ratios concerning that party's (or all independent candidates') votes in House general elections in the district, all federal offices in the state, or for presidential elections in the state (whichever amount was highest);

- Would have established mechanism for candidates to increase their spending limits based on submission of petition signatures (not applicable to candidate with highest limit in the race);

- Payments were to have been made to candidates for election expenses in amounts equal to the expenditure limits calculated above from a Grassroots Good Citizenship Fund, established within the Treasury;

- Fund would have been financed by voluntary taxpayer designations of any refunds owed them of at least $1, plus any additional contributions they wished to make, and by a tax on corporations of 0.1% on taxable income above $10 million;

- Would have directed FEC to make extensive public service announcements from January 15 to April 15 to promote the fund;

- Would have allowed only one other source for campaign expenditures — contributions from national and state political parties, of up to 5% of the applicable spending limit;

- Would have limited spending in non-general House elections (e.g., primaries) to one-third of the general-election spending limit;

- If any part of the act or these amendments were held unconstitutional by the Supreme Court of the United States, would have provided for expedited (fast-track) consideration by Congress of a constitutional amendment to allow reasonable restrictions on contributions, expenditures, and disbursements in federal campaigns; any legislation enacted to enforce such an amendment would have expired four presidential elections after enactment, unless extended by Congress.;

- Unless otherwise specified, legislation would have taken effect in 2007 and expired in 2020.

Other Provisions

- Would have banned independent expenditures in connection with House elections (but would have provided for fast-track consideration of a constitutional amendment to allow reasonable limits if the ban were held unconstitutional);
- Would have banned soft money spending in connection with House elections (but would have provided for fast-track consideration of a constitutional amendment to allow reasonable limits if the ban were held unconstitutional).

H.R. 5281 (Leach) — Campaign Reform Act of 2004

(Introduced May 3, 2006; referred to Committee on House Administration)

Public Finance Provisions

- Would have created House of Representatives Election Campaign Account, within the Presidential Election Campaign Fund, to provide matching payments to eligible House candidates;
- Eligibility would have been established by (1) raising at least $10,000 from individuals in that election cycle; (2) qualifying for the primary or general election ballot; (3) having an opponent in the primary or general election; and (4) limiting receipts and expenditures in election to $500,000 or the aggregate matching payment limit, whichever was greater;
- Would have provided for an equal match of contributions from instate individuals whose aggregate contributions to that candidate for that election did not exceed $500;
- Aggregate matching payments were not to exceed $175,000 in an election, unless (1) a non-eligible opponent raised more than $500,000 for that election, in which case the matching fund payment could have equaled the opponent's receipts; (2) any

opponent in a contested primary raised more than $50,000, in which case the payments could have been increased by up to $75,000; or (3) a runoff occurred, in which case the payments could have been increased by up to $50,000;

- Payments for House candidates were to have come from House of Representatives Election Campaign Account, once Secretary of Treasury determined that there were adequate funds for presidential campaigns, and from supplemental authorizations by Congress.

APPENDIX 3.
PUBLIC FINANCE BILLS IN THE 110TH CONGRESS: SUMMARY OF KEY PROVISIONS

H.R. 1614 (Tierney) — Clean Money, Clean Elections Act of 2007

(Introduced March 20, 2007; jointly referred to Committees on House Administration, Energy and Commerce, Ways and Means, and Oversight and Government Reform)

Public Finance Provisions

- Would establish voluntary public financing system for House candidates;
- Would provide full public subsidies, 30 minutes of free broadcast time in primary and 75 minutes in general election, and additional broadcast time at 50% of lowest unit rate for House candidates who participate in public financing system and spend no private funds beyond subsidy once qualified;
- Would allow candidates, prior to qualification, to raise *seed money* (up to $50,000, in contributions of $100 or less) by raising $5 donations from 1,500 state residents; others would qualify by raising 150% of amount raised by major party candidates;

- Subsidy would equal applicable percentage (60% for general election, 40% for major party candidate in primary, and 25% for other primary candidates) of 80% of base amount per election;
- Base amount would be national average of winning House candidate expenditures in two most recent general elections, but not be less than amount provided in previous election cycle (and would include annual adjustments based on media costs in the state in which the participating candidate is running);
- Would reduce subsidy to 40% of amount otherwise determined for unopposed candidates;
- Would provide additional subsidies to compensate for spending by opponents, opposing independent expenditures, and electioneering communications above specified thresholds;
- Would deny lowest unit rate to non-participating House candidates;
- Would create Clean Elections Review Commission to monitor functioning of House public financing program and make legislative recommendations;
- Would authorize tax credits for contributions to the House Clean Elections Fund, subject to restrictions specified in the bill;
- Would finance benefits from House of Representatives Election Fund using appropriated funds, qualifying contributions, unused seed money, and voluntary donations.

Other Provisions

- In House races with at least one publicly financed candidate, would limit party spending on behalf of a candidate to the lesser of 10% of general election candidate's subsidy or the coordinated party expenditure limit established in FECA[175];
- Would amend "contribution" to include anything of value for purpose of influencing a federal election and that was coordinated with candidate;
- Would set specific reporting requirements for participating and nonparticipating candidates, particularly in final weeks of election or when specified financial thresholds are met;
- Would limit the amount of party coordinated expenditures on behalf of publicly financed candidates;
- Would define "payment made in coordination with a candidate" to include payments (1) in cooperation, consultation or concert with,

or at request or suggestion of a candidate or agent; (2) using candidate-prepared materials; (3) based on information about campaign plans provided by candidate's campaign for purpose of expenditure; (4) by a spender who during that election cycle had acted in an official position for a candidate, in an executive, policymaking, or advisory capacity; and (5) by a spender who had used the same consultants as an affected candidate during election cycle; would have deemed payments made in coordination with a candidate as a "contribution" or "expenditure" (but exempted a payment by a party in coordination with a "clean money" candidate);

- Would require electronic filing of disclosure reports;
- Would prohibit preemption of House campaign broadcast ads, unless beyond broadcasters' control;
- Would prohibit franked mass mailings from 90 days before a primary election period through general election, unless Member is not a candidate or mailing promotes public forum with candidate name only;
- Would authorize imposition of civil penalties for excessive contributions or expenditures (penalty may not exceed 10 times amount of excessive contribution or expenditure);
- Would set specific reporting requirements for participating and nonparticipating candidates, particularly in final weeks of election or when specified financial thresholds are met;
- Includes statement of findings and declarations;
- Would allow FEC to petition Supreme Court;
- If any provision or act of this statute were held unconstitutional, the remainder of act and statute would be unaffected; would provide for direct appeals to the Supreme Court.

H.R. 2817 (Obey) — Let the Public Decide Clean Campaign Act

(Introduced June 21, 2007; referred to Committees on House Administration, Ways and Means, and Rules)

Public Finance Provisions

- Would set mandatory limits on House general election spending based on median household income per district, with a maximum of $2 million for all major party candidates in the wealthiest district; actual amount would be distributed according to the ratio of district-wide votes the nominees of each major-party received in the district during the three most recent general elections;

- In other (non-wealthiest) districts, the "maximum combined expenditures" for major-party candidates would be $2 million minus two-thirds of the percentage difference between the median household incomes in the wealthiest district and the district in question, multiplied by $2 million; actual amount would be distributed according to the ratio of district-wide votes the nominees of each major-party candidate received in the district during the three most recent general elections

- If no elections occurred with two major-party candidates, the vote-ratio for Senate elections during the same period would be used to determine House spending limits noted above;

- Maximum expenditure for minor party or independent candidates would be based on comparable ratios concerning that party's (or all independent candidates') votes in House general elections in the district, all federal offices in the state, or for presidential elections in the state (whichever amount were highest);

- Would establish a mechanism for candidates to increase their spending limits based on submission of specified number of petition signatures (not applicable to candidate with highest limit in the race);

- Would limit House candidates' spending to funds from a proposed Grassroots Good Citizenship Fund, to be established within the U.S. Treasury, and to specified amounts from state and national party committees

- Grassroots Good Citizenship Fund would be financed by voluntary taxpayer contributions (of at least $1) from any refunds owed, plus any additional contributions they wished to make, and by a tax on corporations of 0.1% on taxable income of more than $10 million;

- Would direct FEC to make extensive public service announcements, through time made available by television networks, from January 15 to April 15 to promote the public financing fund;

- Would allow only one other source of campaign expenditures: contributions from national and state political parties, of up to 5% of the candidate's applicable spending limit;
- Would limit spending in non-general House elections (i.e., primaries) to one-third of the general-election spending limit;
- If any part of the act or these amendments were held unconstitutional by the Supreme Court, would provide for expedited consideration by Congress of a constitutional amendment to allow reasonable restrictions on contributions, expenditures, and disbursements in federal campaigns; any legislation enacted to enforce such an amendment would expire four presidential elections after enactment, unless extended by Congress;
- Unless otherwise specified, legislation would take effect in 2009 and expire in 2022.

Other Provisions

- Would ban independent expenditures in connection with House elections (but would provides for expedited consideration of a constitutional amendment to allow reasonable limits if the ban were held unconstitutional);
- Would ban "soft money" spending in connection with House elections (but specifies expedited consideration of a constitutional amendment to allow reasonable limits if the ban were held unconstitutional).

S. 936 (Durbin) — Fair Elections Now Act

(Introduced March 20, 2007; referred to the Committee on Finance)

Public Finance Provisions

- Would establish voluntary public financing system for Senate candidates;
- Would provide full public subsidies, political advertising vouchers up to $100,000 multiplied by the number of congressional districts in the state in which the candidate is running (authority to use vouchers could be transferred to political parties for cash value),

and additional broadcast time at 80% of lowest unit rate for Senate candidates who participate in public financing system and spend no private funds beyond subsidy once qualified;

- Would allow candidates, prior to qualification, to raise *seed money* (up to $75,000 plus $7,500 for each congressional district in the state in excess of one district, in contributions of $100 or less) by raising $5 donations from state residents (number of contributions must be at least equal to the sum of 2,000 plus 500 for each congressional district in the state in excess of one district) others would qualify by raising 150% of amount raised by major party candidates;
- Subsidy would equal applicable percentage (100% for general election, 67% for major party candidate in primary, and 25% for other primary candidates) of base amount per election;
- Base amount would be $750,000 plus $150,000 for each congressional district in the state in excess of one congressional district; base would be adjusted based on state media-market index to be determined by the FEC and FCC; additional indexing would be based on the consumer price index;
- Would reduce subsidy to 25% of amount otherwise determined for unopposed general election candidates;
- Would allow leadership PACs associated with participating candidates to accept contributions from individuals if those contributions did not exceed $100 annually, and disbursements did not benefit the participant's campaign;
- Would create Senate Fair Elections Commission to monitor functioning of House public financing program (including debate functioning compared with similar state requirements for publicly funded candidates) and make legislative recommendations (bill includes provisions for expedited Senate consideration of such recommendations);
- Would authorize tax credits for contributions to the Senate Fair Elections Fund, subject to restrictions specified in the bill;
- Would provide additional subsidies to compensate for spending by opponents, opposing independent expenditures, and electioneering communications above specified thresholds;
- Would finance benefits from Senate Fair Elections fund using proceeds from "recovered spectrum" auctions, spectrum user fees,

voluntary contributions, qualifying contributions, unused seed money, and voluntary donations.

Other Provisions

- In Senate races with at least one publicly financed candidate, would limit party spending on behalf of a candidate to the lesser of 10% of general election candidate's subsidy or the coordinated party expenditure limit established in FECA;[176]
- Includes statement of findings and declarations;
- Would require publicly financed candidates to participate in debates;
- Would extend the lowest unit rate (also known as the "lowest unit charge") to national political party committees;
- Would prohibit preemption of Senate campaign broadcast ads, unless beyond broadcasters' control;
- Would require electronic filing of disclosure reports;
- Would prohibit franked mass mailings from 90 days before a primary election period through general election, unless Member is not a candidate or mailing promotes public forum with candidate name only;
- Would authorize imposition of civil penalties for excessive contributions or expenditures (penalty may not exceed three times amount of excessive contribution or expenditure);
- Would limit the amount of party coordinated expenditures on behalf of publicly financed candidates;
- Would set specific reporting requirements for participating and nonparticipating candidates, particularly in final weeks of election or when specified financial thresholds are met;
- Would allow FEC to petition Supreme Court;
- If any provision of the act were held unconstitutional, the remainder of act and statute would be unaffected;
- Appeals related to the act's constitutionality could be taken directly to the Supreme Court of the United States.

S. 1285 (Durbin) — Fair Elections Now Act

(Introduced May 3, 2007; referred to the Committee on Rules and Administration)

Public Finance Provisions

- Would establish voluntary public financing system for Senate candidates;
- Would provide full public subsidies, political advertising vouchers up to $100,000 multiplied by the number of congressional districts in the state in which the candidate is running (authority to use vouchers could be transferred to political parties for cash value), and additional broadcast time at 80% of lowest unit rate for Senate candidates who participate in public financing system and spend no private funds beyond subsidy once qualified;
- Would allow candidates, prior to qualification, to raise *seed money* (up to $75,000 plus $7,500 for each congressional district in the state in excess of one district, in contributions of $100 or less) by raising $5 donations from state residents (number of contributions must be at least equal to the sum of 2,000 plus 500 for each congressional district in the state in excess of one district) others would qualify by raising 150% of amount raised by major party candidates;
- Subsidy would equal applicable percentage (100% for general election, 67% for major party candidate in primary, and 25% for other primary candidates) of base amount per election;
- Base amount would be $750,000 plus $150,000 for each congressional district in the state in excess of one congressional district; base would be adjusted based on state media-market index to be determined by the FEC and FCC; additional indexing would be based on the consumer price index;
- Would reduce subsidy to 25% of amount otherwise determined for unopposed general election candidates;
- Would allow leadership PACs associated with participating candidates to accept contributions from individuals if those contributions did not exceed $100 annually, and disbursements did not benefit the participant's campaign;

- Would create Senate Fair Elections Commission to monitor functioning of House public financing program (including debate functioning compared with similar state requirements for publicly funded candidates) and make legislative recommendations (bill includes provisions for expedited Senate consideration of such recommendations);
- Would provide additional subsidies to compensate for spending by opponents, opposing independent expenditures, and electioneering communications above specified thresholds;
- Would finance benefits from Senate Fair Elections fund using proceeds from "recovered spectrum" auctions, spectrum user fees, voluntary contributions, qualifying contributions, unused seed money, and voluntary donations.

Other Provisions

- In Senate races with at least one publicly financed candidate, would limit party spending on behalf of a candidate to the lesser of 10% of general election candidate's subsidy or the coordinated party expenditure limit established in FECA;[177]
- Includes statement of findings and declarations;
- Would require publicly financed candidates to participate in debates;
- Would extend the lowest unit rate (also known as the "lowest unit charge") to national political party committees;
- Would prohibit preemption of Senate campaign broadcast ads, unless beyond broadcasters' control;
- Would require electronic filing of disclosure reports;
- Would prohibit franked mass mailings from 90 days before a primary election period through general election, unless Member is not a candidate or mailing promotes public forum with candidate name only;
- Would authorize imposition of civil penalties for excessive contributions or expenditures (penalty may not exceed three times amount of excessive contribution or expenditure);
- Would limit the amount of party coordinated expenditures on behalf of publicly financed candidates;

- Would set specific reporting requirements for participating and nonparticipating candidates, particularly in final weeks of election or when specified financial thresholds are met;
- Would allow FEC to petition Supreme Court;
- If any provision of the act were held unconstitutional, the remainder of act and statute would be unaffected.
- Appeals related to the act's constitutionality could be taken directly to the Supreme Court of the United States.

REFERENCES

[1]   Former CRS specialist Joseph E. Cantor co-authored the original version of this report.

[2]   424 U.S. 1 (1976).

[3]   P.L. 92-178; 85 Stat. 573.

[4]   P.L. 93-443; 86 Stat. 3.

[5]   "Soft money" generally is used to refer to money that may influence federal elections but is raised and spent outside the purview of federal election laws and would be illegal if spent directly on a federal election by a candidate, party, or political action committee (PAC). Prior to enactment of the Bipartisan Campaign Reform Act of 2002 (BCRA), national parties made extensive efforts to raise such money for their state affiliates, partly to boost the national tickets beyond what could be spent directly.

[6]   Strictly speaking, the term "527" refers to a section of the Internal Revenue Code, which provides tax-exempt status to federal, state, and local *political organizations*, as defined in that statute. Although most 527s operating today are also *political committees* operating under federal and state election law, certain groups with 527 status are arguably not being so regulated because their public communications do not contain express advocacy language which has generally been held to be the standard for election law regulation.

[7]   Federal Election Commission, "Presidential Matching Fund Income Tax Checkoff Status," June 2006.

[8]   For a fuller explanation and discussion of the presidential system, see CRS Report RL32786, *The Presidential Election Campaign Fund and*

Tax Checkoff: Background and Current Issues, by Joseph E. Cantor. (This section is excerpted from that report.)

[9] Footnote 65 in *Buckley* stated: "Congress may engage in public financing of election campaigns and may condition acceptance of public funds on an agreement by the candidate to abide by specified expenditure limitations. Just as a candidate may voluntarily limit the size of the contributions he chooses to accept, he may decide to forego private fundraising and accept public funding."

[10] See, for example, Gary C. Jacobson, *Money in Congressional Elections* (New Haven: Yale University Press, 1980), pp. 183-190; Citizens Research Foundation, *New Realities, New Thinking: Report of the Task Force on Campaign Finance Reform*, University of Southern California, 1997, pp. 18-19 (Majority Views).

[11] See, for example: Citizens Research Foundation, *New Realities, New Thinking: Report of the Task Force on Campaign Finance Reform*, University of Southern California, 1997, pp. 16-19 (Majority Views).

[12] Relevant polling and public opinion data are discussed later in this report.

[13] Donald A. Gross and Robert K. Goidel, *The States of Campaign Finance Reform* (Columbus, OH: The Ohio State University Press, 2003), p. 10.

[14] For an overview of some of this testimony, representing support for and opposition to BCRA, see Anthony Corrado, Thomas E. Mann, and Trevor Potter, eds., *Inside the Campaign Finance Battle: Court Testimony on the New Reforms* (Washington: Brookings Institution Press, 2003).

[15] See, for example, Anthony Gierzynski, "A Framework for the Study of Campaign Finance," in Joel A. Thompson and Gary F. Moncrief, eds., *Campaign Finance in State Legislative Elections* (Washington: CQ Press, 1998), p. 21.

[16] John Samples, ed., *Welfare for Politicians? Taxpayer Financing of Campaigns* (Washington: Cato Institute, 2005).

[17] See, for example, Thomas M. Finneran, "The Case Against Taxpayer Financing: A View From Massachusetts," in John Samples, ed., *Welfare for Politicians?* pp. 23-30.

[18] See, for example, Chip Mellor, "Three Lessons from Arizona," in John Samples, ed., *Welfare for Politicians?* p. 38.

[19] See CRS Report RL33580, *Campaign Finance: An Overview*, by Joseph E. Cantor; and Ruth Marcus, "Costliest Race Nears End; Bush,

Gore Running Close; U.S. Campaigns Fuel $3 Billion In Spending," *Washington Post*, November 6, 2000, p. A1.

[20] See, for example, Stephen Ansolabehere, John M. de Figueiredo, and James M. Snyder Jr., "Why is There so Little Money in U.S. Politics?" *The Journal of Economic Perspectives*, vol. 17, no. 1 (winter 2003), pp. 105-130.

[21] Jeffrey Milyo and David Primo, "Reform without Reason? The Scientific Method and Campaign Finance," in *Welfare for Politicians?* pp. 197-211.

[22] Ibid.

[23] Robert E. Mutch, *Campaigns, Congress, and Courts: The Making of Federal Campaign Finance Law* (New York: Praeger, 1988), pp. 42-51; Frank J. Sorauf, *Inside Campaign Finance: Myths and Realities* (New Haven: Yale University Press, 1992), pp. 7-9.

[24] Theodore Roosevelt, "Annual Message of the President of the United States," *Congressional Record*, vol. 42, December 3, 1907, p. 78.

[25] U.S. Congress, Senate Special Committee to Investigate Campaign Expenditures of Presidential, Vice Presidential, and Senatorial Candidates in 1936, *Investigation of Campaign Expenditures in 1936*, report pursuant to S.Res. 225 (74th Cong.) and S.Res. 7 (75th Cong.), 75th Cong., 1st sess., S.Rept. 75-151 (Washington: GPO, 1937).

[26] Mutch, *Campaigns, Congress, and Courts*, p. 36.

[27] Henry Cabot Lodge, Jr., "Investigation of Problems Involved in Federal Financing of Presidential Election Campaigns," *Congressional Record*, vol. 95, July 6, 1949, p. 8888.

[28] Ibid.

[29] Richard Neuberger, "Federal Campaign Contributions to Relieve Officeholders of Private Obligations," *Congressional Record*, vol. 102, February 20, 1956, p. 2855.

[30] Frank Thompson, "Principle of Campaign Contributions by the Federal Government Supported by Theodore Roosevelt, Henry Cabot Lodge, Jr., and David Lawrence," Extensions of Remarks, *Congressional Record*, vol. 102, March 6, 1956, p. 4105.

[31] Alexander Heard, *The Costs of Democracy* (Chapel Hill: University of North Carolina Press, 1960), p. 434.

[32] Richard Neuberger, "Federal Campaign Contributions to Relieve Officeholders of Private Obligations," *Congressional Record*, vol. 102, February 20, 1956, p. 2854.

[33] Ibid.

[34] Ibid., p. 2857.

[35]   Ibid., p. 2858.

[36]   43 Stat. 1070.

[37]   U.S. President's Commission on Campaign Costs, *Financing Presidential Elections; Report* (Washington: GPO, 1964).

[38]   Ibid., p. 31-32.

[39]   U.S. Congress, Senate Committee on Finance, *Honest Elections Act of 1967, etc.*, report to accompany H.R. 4890, S.Rept. 90-714, 90th Cong., 1st sess. (Washington: GPO, 1967).

[40]   "Federal Election Campaign Act Amendments of 1973," Debate and Vote in the Senate, *Congressional Record*, vol. 119, July 26, 1973, p. 26115.

[41]   "Temporary Increase in Public Debt Limit," Debate and Vote in the Senate, *Congressional Record*, vol. 119, November 27, 1973, p. 38231.

[42]   Ibid., p. 38240.

[43]   "Disagreeing to Senate Amendments to H.R. 11104, Public Debt Limit," Debate and Vote in the House, *Congressional Record*, vol. 119, November 29, 1973, p. 38680.

[44]   Senate Twice Votes Campaign Financing Reform, *Congressional Quarterly Almanac, 1973* (Washington: Congressional Quarterly, Inc., 1974), vol. 29, p. 754.

[45]   General election funding in presidential elections had been enacted by the Revenue Act of 1971, but the formula was changed in this legislation.

[46]   U.S. Congress, Senate Committee on Rules and Administration, *Federal Election Campaign Act Amendments of 1974*, report to accompany S. 3044, 93rd Cong., 2nd sess., S.Rept. 93-689 (Washington: GPO, 1974).

[47]   Ibid., p. 4-5.

[48]   "Federal Election Campaign Act Amendments of 1974," Debate and Vote in the Senate, *Congressional Record*, vol. 120, April 11, 1974, p. 10952.

[49]   "Federal Election Campaign Act Amendments of 1974," Debate and Vote in the House, *Congressional Record*, vol. 120, August 8, 1974, p. 27490.

[50]   Those spending limits were declared unconstitutional by *Buckley v. Valeo* in 1976.

[51]   P.L. 93-443.

[52] "Federal Election Campaign Act Amendments of 1976," Debate and Vote in the House, *Congressional Record*, vol. 122, April 1, 1976, p. 9096.

[53] "Public Financing," *CQ Almanac: 95th Congress, 1st Session, 1977* (Washington: Congressional Quarterly, Inc., 1978), vol. 33, p. 805.

[54] "Public Financing of Senate Elections," Debate and Vote in the Senate, *Congressional Record*, vol. 123, August 2, 1977, pp. 26022-26023.

[55] U.S. Congress, House Committee on House Administration, *Public Financing of Congressional Elections*, hearings, 95th Cong., 1st sess., May 18, 19; June 21, 23, 28; July 12, 1977 (Washington: GPO, 1977).

[56] "Public Financing," *CQ Almanac, 1977*, pp. 807-808.

[57] Rhodes Cook, "Bill Lowering Spending Levels Reported," *Congressional Quarterly Weekly Reports*, vol. 36, March 18, 1978, p. 718.

[58] "Providing for Consideration of H.R. 11315, Federal Election Campaign Act Amendments of 1978," Debate and Vote in the House, *Congressional Record*, vol. 124, March 21, 1978, pp. 7879-7880.

[59] "Public Financing, Campaign Spending Bills," *CQ Almanac: 95th Congress, 2nd Session, 1978* (Washington: Congressional Quarterly, Inc., 1979), vol. 34, p. 771.

[60] "Providing for Consideration of H.R. 11983, Federal Election Commission Authorization, Fiscal Year 1979," Debate and Vote in the House, *Congressional Record*, vol. 124, July 19, 1978, p. 21715.

[61] U.S. Congress, House Committee on House Administration, *Public Financing of Congressional Elections*, hearings on H.R. 1 and related legislation, 96th Cong., 1st sess., March 15, 20-22, 27, 1979 (Washington: GPO, 1979).

[62] "Public Campaign Funds," *CQ Almanac: 96th Congress, 1st Session, 1979* (Washington: Congressional Quarterly, Inc., 1980), vol. 35, pp. 553-556.

[63] This changed late in the 99th Congress, on August 12, 1986, when the Senate passed the Boren-Goldwater amendment to curb PACs, although no further action was taken.

[64] U.S. Congress, Senate Committee on Rules and Administration, *Senatorial Election Campaign Act of 1987*, report to accompany S. 2, 100th Cong., 1st sess., S.Rept. 100-58 (Washington: GPO, 1987).

[65] Between June 3, 1987, and February 26, 1988, eight unsuccessful cloture votes occurred on June 9, 16, 17, 18, 19, September 10, 15, 1987, and February 26, 1988.

[66] U.S. Congress, Senate Committee on Rules and Administration, *Senatorial Election Campaign Act of 1989,* report to accompany S. 137, 101st Cong., 2nd sess., S.Rept. 101-253 (Washington: GPO, 1990).

[67] "Senatorial Elections Campaign Act," Debate and Vote in the Senate, *Congressional Record*, vol. 136, July 30, 1990, p. 20329.

[68] Ibid., July 31, 1990, p. 20659.

[69] Ibid., August 1, 1990, p. 21074; the bill also included bans on PACs, party soft money, and bundling, and curbs on out-of-state money and tax-exempt groups.

[70] "Campaign Cost Reduction and Reform Act of 1990," Debate and Vote in the House, *Congressional Record*, vol. 136, August 3, 1990, pp. 22251-22252.

[71] U.S. Congress, Senate Committee on Rules and Administration, *Senate Election Ethics Act of 1991,* report to accompany S. 3, 102nd Cong., 1st sess., S.Rept. 102-37 (Washington: GPO, 1991).

[72] "Senate Election Ethics Act, Debate and Vote in the Senate," *Congressional Record*, vol. 137, May 22, 1991, p. 11937.

[73] Ibid., p. 11979.

[74] Ibid., May 23, 1991, p. 12355.

[75] It also included bans on PACs, bundling (discussed below), and party soft money; tax-exempt group curbs; a requirement that candidates appear in broadcast ads; and a ban on post-election repayments of candidate loans. S. 137 incorporated such floor amendments as an honoraria ban, earned and unearned income limits, and debate requirements for publicly funded presidential races.

[76] U.S. Congress, House Committee on House Administration, *House of Representatives Campaign Spending Limit and Election Reform Act of 1991,* report to accompany H.R. 3750, 102nd Cong., 1st sess., H.Rept. 102-340 (Washington: GPO, 1991).

[77] U.S. Congress, House Committee on Rules, *Providing for Consideration of H.R. 3750,* report to accompany H.Res. 299, 102nd Cong., 1st sess., H.Rept.102-365 (Washington: GPO, 1991).

[78] "Two Campaign Finance Bills Passed," *CQ Almanac: 102nd Congress, 1st Session, 1991* (Washington: Congressional Quarterly, Inc., 1992), vol. 47, p. 21.

[79] "House of Representatives Campaign Spending Limit and Election Reform Act of 1991," Debate and Vote in the House, *Congressional Record*, vol. 137, November 25, 1991, pp. 34708-34709.

[80]   H.R. 3750 also included an aggregate cap on PAC and large donor receipts, a leadership PAC ban, curbs on party soft money, and a ban on independent expenditures by lobbyists.

[81]   U.S. Congress, Conference Committee, *Congressional Campaign Spending Limit and Election Reform Act of 1992,* report to accompany S. 3, 102nd Cong., 2nd sess., H.Rept. 102-479 and H.Rept. 102-487 (Washington: GPO, 1992).

[82]   Bundling refers to the collection of campaign funds for a candidate by an intermediary (who is not an agent of the campaign) in amounts beyond what he or she could legally donate to that candidate.

[83]   "Conference Report on S. 3, Congressional Campaign Spending Limit and Election Reform Act of 1992," Debate and Vote in the House, *Congressional Record*, vol. 138, April 9, 1992, p. 9023.

[84]   "Senate Election Ethics Act — Conference Report," Debate and Vote in the Senate, *Congressional Record*, vol. 138, April 30, 1992, p. 9964.

[85]   U.S. National Archives and Records Administration, Office of the Federal Register, *Public Papers of the President of the United States: George Bush, 1992-1993*, vol. 1 (Washington: GPO, 1993), pp. 736-737.

[86]   "Disapproval of S. 3 — The Congressional Campaign Spending Limit and Election Reform Act of 1992," Debate and Vote in the Senate, *Congressional Record*, vol. 138, May 13, 1992, p. 11146.

[87]   U.S. Congress, Senate Committee on Rules and Administration, *Congressional Spending Limit and Election Reform Act of 1993,* report to accompany S. 3, 103rd Cong., 1st sess., S.Rept. 103-41 (Washington: GPO, 1993).

[88]   U.S. National Archives and Records Administration, Office of the Federal Register, *Public Papers of the President of the United States: William J. Clinton, 1993*, vol. 1 (Washington: GPO, 1994), pp. 584-589.

[89]   "Congressional Campaign Spending Limit and Election Reform Act of 1993," Debate and Vote in the Senate, *Congressional Record*, vol. 139, June 16, 1993, p. 12952.

[90]   Ibid., June 17, 1993, p. 13246.

[91]   U.S. Congress, House Committee on House Administration, *House of Representatives Campaign Spending Limit and Election Reform Act of 1993,* report to accompany H.R. 3, 103rd Cong., 1st sess., H.Rept. 103-375 (Washington: GPO, 1993).

[92] "House of Representatives Campaign Spending Limit and Election Reform Act of 1993," Debate and Vote in the House, *Congressional Record*, vol. 139, November 22, 1993, pp. 31792-31793.

[93] "House of Representatives Campaign Spending Limit and Election Reform Act of 1993," Debate and Vote in the Senate, *Congressional Record*, vol. 140, September 30, 1994, p. 26962.

[94] S. 936, sec. 502 (pp. 10-11) of S. 936 as introduced in the Senate, according to the Legislative Information System (LIS). See also sec. 111 (p. 48) in ibid. On spectrum auctions, CRS Report RL31764, *Spectrum Management: Auctions*, by Linda K. Moore.

[95] H.R. 2817 sets spending limits for primary elections, but only specifies a public financing system for general elections. By contrast, H.R. 1614, S. 936, and S. 1285 propose public financing systems for both primary and general elections.

[96] On expedited procedures, see CRS Report RS20234, *Expedited or "Fast-Track" Legislative Procedures*, by Christopher M. Davis, and CRS Report 98-888 GOV, *"Fast-Track" or Expedited Procedures: Their Purposes, Elements, and Implications*, by Christopher M. Davis.

[97] On constitutional issues surrounding campaign finance legislation, see CRS Report RL30669, *Campaign Finance Regulation Under the First Amendment: Buckley v. Valeo and Its Supreme Court Progeny*, by L. Paige Whitaker.

[98] Letter from David K. Rehr, president and chief executive officer, National Association of Broadcasters, to Hon. Dianne Feinstein, Chairman, Senate Committee on Rules and Administration, June 20, 2007.

[99] See, for example, Gary C. Jacobson, *Money in Congressional Elections*, pp. 183-190; Citizens Research Foundation, *New Realities, New Thinking: Report of the Task Force on Campaign Finance Reform*, pp. 18-19 (Majority Views).

[100] David W. Adamany and George E. Agree, *Political Money: A Strategy for Campaign Financing in America* (Baltimore: The Johns Hopkins University Press, 1975), pp. 179-180.

[101] See CRS Report RS21716, *Political Organizations Under Section 527 of the Internal Revenue Code*, by Erika Lunder.

[102] U.S. Congress, Senate Committee on Rules and Administration, *Congressional Spending Limit and Election Reform Act of 1993*, report to accompany S. 3, 103rd Cong., 1st sess., S.Rept. 103-41 (Washington: GPO, 1993), p. 40.

[103] Public Campaign, "Annotated Model Legislation for Clean Money/Clean Elections Reform" at [http://www.publicampaign.org/modelbill].

[104] According to Public Campaign, in the previously cited material, "Revenue for the Clean Money/Clean Elections Fund could come from some combination of these and other sources: the qualifying contributions collected by participating candidates, an income tax check-off system (similar to the one in place for presidential elections), a highly publicized program of voluntary contributions, and direct government appropriations to make up the balance of what is needed. The Clean Money/Clean Elections program could be offset (thus requiring no tax increase) by the elimination of unnecessary tax exemptions and other subsidies previously granted to major campaign contributors. It is estimated that such subsidies currently cost taxpayers far more than what it would cost to provide full public financing under a Clean Money/Clean Elections system."

[105] Donald A. Gross and Robert K. Goidel, *The States of Campaign Finance Reform* , p. 5.

[106] David Schultz, ed., *Money, Politics, and Campaign Finance Reform Law in the States* (Durham, NC: Carolina Academic Press, 2002), p. 19.

[107] CRS obtained information about states' public financing programs from various academic publications, publications from independent research organizations, interest groups, and consultations with individual scholars and researchers. Jennifer Drage Bowser at the National Conference of State Legislatures, and Steven M. Levin at the Center for Governmental Studies provided helpful background information. Several academic researchers also provided extensive consultations about public financing and potential data sources. Sources appear in table notes accompanying **Table 1**. In some cases, consulted sources included organizations or scholars who have publicly supported or opposed public financing. Also, sources sometimes provided different accounts of public financing in each state. CRS contacted campaign finance officials in the states listed in **Table 1** to clarify cases of incomplete or contradictory information found in other sources. Notes accompanying **Table 1** provide additional information about alternative interpretations from other sources. The number of states offering "public financing" depends on how the term is defined, and whether assistance to candidates or candidates *and* parties is included. For example, according to a 2006

media account, seven states offer public financing, although the definition of "public financing" or source for this information was not provided. See Elana Schor, "GOP Senator eyes public financing bill," *The Hill*, February 22, 2006, p. 3. By contrast, Public Citizen suggests that "14 states, and 13 local jurisdictions provide some form of public financing of candidate campaigns, with these numbers, especially at the local level, regularly in flux." See "Public Financing of Non-Presidential Campaigns," fact sheet, n.d., at [http://www.citizen.org/ congress/campaign/issues/pub_fin/index.cfm?ID=11062& relatedpages=1&catID=106&secID=1067]. A 2006 report by the Center for Governmental Studies noted that "different forms" of public financing exist in "25 states and 13 local jurisdictions." See Steven M. Levin, *Keeping It Clean: Public Financing in American Elections* (Los Angeles: Center for Governmental Studies, 2006), p. x. A 2005 Common Cause analysis identified 14 states that "provide direct public financing to candidates," and 10 others that "provide minimal public financing to candidates and/or political parties." See "Public Financing in the States" at [http://www.commoncause.org/ site/pp.asp?c=dkLNK1MQIwG&b=507399].

[108] This report uses the terms "clean money" and "clean elections" in reference to the interest group Public Campaign's title for its public financing model. The terms are also widely used in state public financing laws and in general campaign finance parlance. The U.S. General Accounting Office (now the Government Accountability Office) has taken a similar approach in using the term "clean elections" in its research. See U.S. General Accounting Office, *Campaign Finance Reform: Early Experiences of Two States That Offer Full Public Funding for Political Candidates*, GAO-03-453, May 2003, p. 79, footnote 4. This CRS report takes no position on whether such labels are appropriate.

[109] Exceptions vary by state. In some cases, third-party or independent candidates are not eligible for as much funding as are major-party candidates.

[110] Public Campaign, "About Us" at [http://www.publiccampaign.org/ about/index.htm].

[111] New Jersey falls into both categories — clean money and other — because the state offers non-Clean Money funding for gubernatorial campaigns, and Clean Money funding to legislative candidates participating in a pilot public financing program.

[112] For an overview of the maximum public funding allowed in the states, see Steven M. Levin, *Keeping It Clean: Public Financing in American Elections*, "State Table 3."

[113] This information is based on consultations with staff at Michigan's Campaign Finance Division (telephone conversation with R. Sam Garrett, August 2, 2006).

[114] Telephone conversations between R. Sam Garrett and Jared DeMarinis, Maryland Director of Candidacy and Campaign Finance, June 30, 2006, and August 24, 2006. The amount is subject to annual adjustments.

[115] Telephone conversation between R. Sam Garrett and Frank Daley, Executive Director of the Nebraska Accountability and Disclosure Commission, July 31, 2006. For a brief discussion of Nebraska's program, see also Michael J. Malbin and Thomas L. Gais, eds., *The Day After Reform: Sobering Campaign Finance Lessons from the American States* (Albany, NY: The Rockefeller Institute Press, 1998), p. 60.

[116] Donald A. Gross, Robert K. Goidel, and Todd G. Shields, "State Campaign Finance Regulations and Electoral Competition," *American Politics Research*, vol. 30, no. 2 (March 2002), pp. 143-145; see also Michael J. Malbin and Thomas L. Gais, eds., *The Day After Reform*.

[117] For an example of the difficulty in standardizing measures of public financing in campaign finance research, see Christopher Witko, "Measuring the Stringency of State Campaign Finance Regulation," *State Politics and Policy Quarterly*, vol. 5, no. 3 (fall 2005), pp. 297-298. See also Michael J. Malbin and Thomas L. Gais, eds., *The Day After Reform*, chapter 4.

[118] Kenneth R. Mayer, Timothy Werner, and Amanda Williams, "Public Funding Programs and Competition," in Michael P. McDonald and John Samples, eds., *The Marketplace of Democracy: Electoral Competition and American Politics* (Washington: Cato Institute and Brookings Institution Press, 2006), p. 246.

[119] On its own, however, public financing limits only candidate spending — not spending by outside groups such as parties, interest groups, and 527 organizations.

[120] Joel A. Thompson and Gary F. Moncrief, eds., *Campaign Finance in State Legislative Elections*, p. 112. These findings are based on evidence from only two states —Minnesota and Wisconsin — because they were "the only states that allowed significant public financing of state legislative elections at the time of this study," which was

published in 1998. See Joel A. Thompson and Gary F. Moncrief, eds., *Campaign Finance in State Legislative Elections*, p. 112.

[121] For example, Kenneth Mayer and John Wood found that public financing reduced campaign costs in Wisconsin, but generally did not foster closer elections. See Kenneth R. Mayer and John M. Wood, "The Impact of Public Financing on Electoral Competitiveness: Evidence from Wisconsin, 1964-1990," *Legislative Studies Quarterly*, vol. 20, no. 1 (February 1995), pp. 69-88. A study of gubernatorial elections from 1978-1998 found that although public financing provided to *political parties* led to *higher* gubernatorial campaign costs, public financing provided directly to *candidate campaigns* led to *lower*-cost gubernatorial races. Neither result was statistically significant, however, and the authors cautioned that their findings on this point were "not definitive." See Donald A. Gross and Robert K. Goidel, *The States of Campaign Finance Reform*, p. 49.

[122] Ibid, p. 111.

[123] As the authors noted, however, their definition of "competitiveness" is "not a universally accepted threshold." They used a vote-margin between candidates of no more than 20% to mark "competitive" elections. See Kenneth R. Mayer, Timothy Werner, and Amanda Williams, "Public Funding Programs and Competition," in Michael P. McDonald and John Samples, eds. *The Marketplace of Democracy: Electoral Competition and American Politics*, p. 259.

[124] See, for example, Donald A. Gross and Robert K. Goidel, *The States of Campaign Finance Reform*, p. 73; and Patrick D. Donnay and Graham P. Ramsden, "Public Financing of Legislative Elections: Lessons from Minnesota," *Legislative Studies Quarterly*, vol. 20, no. 3 (August 1995), pp. 351-364. On arguments that public financing favors Democrats and incumbents, see Steven M. Levin, *Keeping It Clean: Public Financing in American Elections*, p. 16.

[125] Kenneth R. Mayer, Timothy Werner, and Amanda Williams, "Public Funding Programs and Competition," pp. 263-265. On Wisconsin, see also Kenneth R. Mayer and John M. Wood, "The Impact of Public Financing on Electoral Competitiveness: Evidence from Wisconsin, 1964-1990," pp. 69-88.

[126] Steven M. Levin, *Keeping It Clean: Public Financing in American Elections*, p. xi.

[127] Peter L. Francia and Paul S. Herrnson, "The Impact of Public Finance Laws on Fundraising in State Legislative Election," *American Politics Research*, vol. 31, no. 5 (September 2003), p. 535.

[128] David B. Magleby and Candice J. Nelson, *The Money Chase: Congressional Campaign Finance Reform* (Washington: Brookings Institution, 1990).

[129] Ibid.

[130] "Leadership PACs" are committees that are technically independent from legislators, but are generally established by and at least unofficially linked with those legislators. These committees are legally distinct from a legislator's personal campaign committee. At the federal level, "Leadership PACs traditionally have been used by legislative leaders to contribute to the campaigns of other members of Congress as a way of gaining a party majority and earning the gratitude of their colleagues or as a way of financing nationwide political activity by party leaders." See Trevor Potter, "The Current State of Campaign Finance Law," in Anthony Corrado, Thomas E. Mann, Daniel R. Ortiz, and Trevor Potter, *The New Campaign Finance Sourcebook* (Washington: Brookings Institution Press, 2005), p. 52.

[131] Steven M. Levin, *Keeping It Clean: Public Financing in American Elections*, p. xi.

[132] Ibid.

[133] U.S. General Accounting Office, *Campaign Finance Reform: Early Experiences of Two States That Offer Full Public Funding for Political Candidates*, p. 83.

[134] P.L. 107-155; 116 Stat. 81.

[135] U.S. General Accounting Office, *Campaign Finance Reform: Early Experiences of Two States That Offer Full Public Funding for Political Candidates*, "Highlights" page. Regarding outside critiques of the GAO report, see Kenneth R. Mayer, Timothy Werner, and Amanda Williams, "Public Funding Programs and Competition," pp. 252-255.

[136] U.S. General Accounting Office, *Campaign Finance Reform: Early Experiences of Two States That Offer Full Public Funding for Political Candidates*, "Highlights" page.

[137] For a summary of findings in each of these five research areas, see U.S. General Accounting Office, *Campaign Finance Reform: Early Experiences of Two States That Offer Full Public Funding for Political Candidates*, pp. 4-6.

[138] Ibid., p. 4.

[139] Kenneth R. Mayer, Timothy Werner, and Amanda Williams, "Public Funding Programs and Competition," p. 257. In discussing this

increase, the authors noted, "While we cannot attribute this shift entirely to public funding,...it is likely to have played a key role." Ibid.

[140] Donald A. Gross and Robert K. Goidel, *The States of Campaign Finance Reform*, p. 103; and Patrick Basham and Martin Zelder, "Does Cleanliness Lead to Competitiveness? The Failure of Maine's Experiment," in John Samples, ed., *Welfare for Politicians?* pp. 73-105.

[141] U.S. General Accounting Office, *Campaign Finance Reform: Early Experiences of Two States That Offer Full Public Funding for Political Candidates*, p. 3.

[142] Ibid., pp. 12-13.

[143] "Demographics: 2004 Election," table posted on the Arizona Citizens Clean Elections Commission website at [http://www.ccec.state.az.us/ccecweb/ccecays/docs/20002004DEMOGRAPHICS.pdf]. The CRS authors computed the 56% figure based on data in the table.

[144] U.S. General Accounting Office, *Campaign Finance Reform: Early Experiences of Two States That Offer Full Public Funding for Political Candidates*, pp. 12-13.

[145] Maine Commission on Governmental Ethics and Election Practices, "Maine Clean Election Act Overview," document provided via e-mail to the CRS authors by Nathaniel T. Brown, Candidate Registrar, Commission on Governmental Ethics and Election Practices, September 7, 2006.

[146] Maine Commission on Governmental Ethics and Election Practices, "Maine Clean Election Act Overview: 2004 Participation Update," document provided via e-mail to the CRS authors by Nathaniel T. Brown, Candidate Registrar, Commission on Governmental Ethics and Election Practices, January 11, 2007.

[147] Ibid.; Maine Commission on Governmental Ethics and Election Practices, "Maine Clean Election Act Overview," provided September 7, 2006; and, for 2006 primary data, e-mail to the CRS authors by Nathaniel T. Brown, Candidate Registrar, Commission on Governmental Ethics and Election Practices, January 12, 2007.

[148] This information came from Michael Becker, Voter Education Manager at the Citizens Clean Elections Commission (telephone conversation with R. Sam Garrett, January 9, 2007).

[149] Ibid., p. 26.

[150] Ibid., p. 28.

[151] For an overview of these arguments, see, for example, Chip Mellor, "Three Lessons from Arizona," in John Samples, ed., *Welfare for Politicians*? pp. 31-47.

[152] Ibid., p. 32-33.

[153] Robert J. Franciosi, "Elections in Arizona, Clean and Unclean," in John Samples, ed., *Welfare for Politicians*? p. 58.

[154] Steven M. Levin, *Keeping It Clean: Public Financing in American Elections*, p. xiii.

[155] Ray J. La Raja and Matthew Saradjian, "Clean Elections: An Evaluation of Public Funding for Maine Legislative Contests," Center for Public Policy and Administration, University of Massachusetts, n.d., at [http://www.masspolicy.org/pdf/WP2004_2.pdf].

[156] Ibid.

[157] Anthony Gierznski, *Money Rules: Financing Elections in America* (Boulder, CO: Westview Press, 2000), pp. 50-51.

[158] Ibid., pp. 4-5.

[159] Ibid., p. 9; and John Samples, ed., *Welfare for Politicians*? pp. 8-9.

[160] Stephen R. Weissman and Ruth A. Hassan, "Public Opinion Polls Concerning Public Financing of Federal Elections 1972-2000: A Critical Analysis and Proposed Future Directions," (Washington: Campaign Finance Institute, 2005), pp. 2-3, at [http://www.cfinst.org/ presidential/report2/pdf/PublicFunding_Surveys.pdf].

[161] Ibid., p. 4.

[162] Ibid., pp. 3-4. The poll reportedly varied in how often each office was mentioned.

[163] Survey information gathered from Polling the Nations Survey Database at [http://poll.orspub.com/]. Search conducted by CRS Information Professional Zina Watkins, May 2006.

[164] Ibid.

[165] Ibid.

[166] Ibid.

[167] Ibid.

[168] Ibid.

[169] The models discussed here are not the only potential avenues for delivering public financing, although they are the mechanisms the states and the presidential system currently use. Other options, such as the "Patriot dollars" program of partial public financing, in which voters would receive small amounts of funds to be distributed to their favored candidates via a blind trust, or subsidies for political parties or to purchase broadcast time, are also possibilities. Yale University law

professors Bruce Ackerman and Ian Ayres proposed the "Patriot dollars" approach in their book *Voting with Dollars*. See Bruce Ackerman and Ian Ayres, *Voting with Dollars: A New Paradigm for Campaign Finance* (New Haven: Yale University Press, 2002).

[170] Some combination of these two approaches might also be possible. However, most programs offering contingency funds for those facing high spending by opponents assume that those opponents do not participate in public financing.

[171] This assumes that "effectiveness" is signaled by high levels of candidate participation.

[172] Richard Briffault, "Public Funding and Democratic Elections," *University of Pennsylvania Law Review*, vol. 148 (1999-2000), p. 585. The quotation above omits Briffault's footnote 70.

[173] See Kenneth R. Mayer and John M. Wood, "The Impact of Public Financing on Electoral Competitiveness," p. 86.

[174] Provisions in *italics* represent contingency provisions, which would have taken effect only under certain specified circumstances.

[175] 2 U.S.C §441a(d)(3)(B). This limit is adjusted based on the consumer price index.

[176] 2 U.S.C §441a(d)(3)(B). This limit is adjusted based on the consumer price index.

[177] 2 U.S.C §441a(d)(3)(B). This limit is adjusted based on the consumer price index.

INDEX

A

academic, 7, 105
access, 8, 14, 15, 57, 58
accounting, 31, 40
administrators, 67
advertisements, 39, 71, 73
advertising, 9, 31, 33, 37, 38, 56, 67, 79, 91, 94
advocacy, 3, 28, 66, 97
age, 34, 71, 78
agent, 81, 89, 103
aid, vii
alternative(s), 27, 105
amendments, 5, 18, 19, 20, 21, 22, 25, 83, 91, 102
appendix, 2
appropriations, 12, 18, 31, 44, 54, 55, 105
argument, 9
Arizona, 43, 45, 48, 53, 58, 59, 60, 61, 65, 98, 110, 111
ash, 55
assessment, 56
atmosphere, 14, 22
attacks, 30
attention, 1, 16, 59
attitudes, 63
Attorney General, 48, 50, 51, 52, 53, 54

authority, 82, 91, 94
availability, 30
awareness, 60

B

background information, 105
banks, 80
benefits, viii, 1, 2, 5, 6, 12, 23, 24, 25, 26, 27, 28, 29, 30, 33, 34, 35, 36, 39, 41, 44, 81, 88, 92, 95
bipartisan, 7
Bipartisan Campaign Reform Act (BCRA), 7, 8, 28, 38, 60, 80, 97, 98
Bipartisan Campaign Reform Act of 2002, 7, 97
breeding, 14
bribery, 15
broadcast media, 68
broadcasters, 24, 33, 37, 38, 79, 82, 89, 93, 95
Buckley v. Valeo, vii, 1, 2, 5, 8, 100, 104
bundling, 26, 80, 102, 103
business, 20

C

California, 98

campaign costs, 6, 7, 9, 24, 37, 38, 44, 63, 108

campaign finance, vii, 13, 16, 18, 21, 23, 25, 28, 54, 55, 57, 63, 64, 104, 105, 106, 107

campaign funds, vii, 13, 15, 103

campaign spending limits, 1, 2, 12, 23, 37

campaigns, vii, 2, 3, 8, 12, 13, 14, 15, 17, 18, 23, 24, 30, 34, 36, 37, 40, 43, 46, 47, 55, 57, 58, 59, 61, 63, 64, 65, 66, 67, 68, 82, 84, 85, 91, 98, 106, 108, 109

candidates, vii, viii, 2, 3, 4, 5, 6, 7, 8, 9, 11, 12, 15, 16, 17, 19, 20, 21, 23, 24, 25, 26, 27, 29, 30, 31, 32, 33, 34, 35, 36, 37, 38, 39, 40, 41, 43, 44, 45, 46, 47, 48, 49, 50, 52, 53, 54, 55, 56, 57, 58, 59, 60, 61, 64, 65, 66, 67, 68, 69, 70, 77, 79, 80, 81, 82, 83, 84, 85, 87, 88, 89, 90, 91, 92, 93, 94, 95, 96, 102, 105, 106, 108, 111

capacity, 81, 89

case study, 2

cast(ing), 16, 39

CBS, 64

certainty, 57

clean money, 29, 44, 45, 46, 53, 59, 60, 65, 66, 80, 81, 89, 106

clients, 63

cloture, 20, 21, 23, 24, 27, 28, 101

commercial, 9, 38

Committee on Rules and Administration, 14, 30, 33, 94, 100, 101, 102, 103, 104

communication, 24, 25, 26, 27, 41, 71, 73, 75, 78

community, 6, 34

competition, 6, 7, 8, 34, 57, 58, 60, 61

competitiveness, 8, 34, 67, 108

complexity, 66

components, 45, 65, 68

concentrates, 66

conditioning, 35

confidence, 3, 4, 46

congress, vii, viii, 1, 2, 5, 7, 11, 12, 13, 15, 16, 17, 18, 19, 20, 21, 22, 23, 24, 25, 26, 27, 28, 29, 30, 31, 32, 33, 34, 36, 37, 38, 40, 41, 45, 65, 66, 67, 68, 69, 70, 71, 72, 73, 74, 75, 76, 77, 78, 79, 83, 85, 87, 91, 98, 99, 100, 101, 102, 103, 104, 106, 109

Congressional Budget Office (CBO), 40, 41

congressional elections, vii, viii, 1, 2, 5, 11, 17, 19, 20, 21, 22, 23, 25, 28, 41, 64, 67, 68

congressional races, 4, 67

Congressional Record, 99, 100, 101, 102, 103, 104

Connecticut, 43, 45, 48, 53, 59

consensus, 21, 28

constitutional, 5, 8, 29, 32, 83, 84, 91, 104

consultants, 81, 89

consumer goods, 9

consumer price index, 31, 92, 94, 112

contingency, 24, 27, 48, 49, 51, 112

control, 23, 28, 82, 89, 93, 95

coordination, 31, 81, 88

corporations, 12, 80, 83, 90

corrosive, 3

corruption, vii, 7, 9, 14, 46

costs, vii, 6, 7, 8, 9, 21, 24, 29, 30, 37, 38, 39, 40, 44, 57, 63, 66, 79, 88, 108

Court of Appeals, 51, 52

coverage, 35

credit, 25, 26, 30, 37, 56, 72

cycles, 31, 60, 68

D

danger, 13

debt, 19

decisions, 3, 35, 37, 40, 41, 46, 66

definition, 30, 106, 108

Democrat(s), 4, 23, 25, 26, 32, 58, 61, 108

density, 37, 38
Department of State, 54
dichotomy, 6
disbursement, 31, 67
disclosure, vii, 5, 12, 18, 80, 82, 89, 93, 95
disputes, 58
distribution, 41
divergence, 3
diversity, 65
donations, 4, 16, 17, 26, 27, 29, 31, 36, 37, 48, 59, 70, 71, 79, 80, 87, 88, 92, 93, 94, 95
donors, 25, 58
dream, 15
duties, 59

E

education, 32, 51, 53, 110
egalitarian, 3
election, 2, 3, 4, 6, 12, 13, 14, 16, 18, 19, 20, 21, 23, 25, 28, 29, 31, 32, 34, 35, 36, 39, 41, 46, 50, 55, 56, 57, 59, 60, 61, 65, 66, 68, 71, 72, 73, 74, 75, 76, 77, 78, 79, 80, 81, 82, 83, 84, 87, 88, 89, 90, 91, 92, 93, 94, 95, 96, 97, 98, 100, 102
electoral process, 34
electronic, 82, 89, 93, 95
employees, 80
environment, 23
evidence, 9, 58, 59, 60, 68, 82, 107
evil, 14
exclusion, 27, 40, 77
expenditures, vii, 3, 5, 9, 13, 16, 19, 24, 25, 26, 27, 30, 31, 32, 33, 34, 35, 37, 38, 39, 40, 41, 56, 58, 60, 61, 66, 71, 73, 74, 75, 76, 77, 78, 80, 81, 83, 84, 88, 89, 90, 91, 92, 93, 95, 103
experts, 7
eyes, 106

F

failure, 23
fairness, 37
faith, 68
family, 20, 35, 71, 73, 75, 77
fear, 8, 66
fears, 9
federal budget, 41
Federal Communications Commission (FCC), 31, 92, 94
federal election activities, 80
Federal Election Campaign Act, 3, 100, 101
Federal Election Commission (FEC), 4, 7, 22, 30, 31, 32, 33, 67, 80, 82, 83, 89, 90, 92, 93, 94, 96, 97, 101
federal elections, vii, 11, 13, 17, 19, 64, 97
federal funds, 16, 24
federal government, 18, 37, 38, 64
federal law, 80
Federal Register, 103
fees, 31, 33, 41, 44, 48, 49, 51, 52, 54, 55, 56, 61, 92, 95
finance(ing), vii, viii, 1, 2, 3, 4, 5, 6, 7, 8, 9, 11, 12, 13, 14, 15, 16, 17, 18, 19, 20, 21, 22, 23, 24, 25, 26, 28, 29, 30, 31, 32, 33, 34, 37, 38, 39, 40, 43, 44, 45, 46, 47, 50, 51, 52, 53, 54, 55, 56, 57, 58, 59, 60, 61, 63, 64, 65, 66, 67, 68, 80, 87, 88, 90, 91, 92, 94, 95, 98, 104, 105, 106, 107, 108, 109, 111, 112
financial resources, 8
financial support, 61
fines, 44, 48, 49, 51, 54, 55, 61
First Amendment, 104
focusing, 18, 37, 63
fraud, 17
frustration, 23
funding, vii, viii, 3, 4, 5, 6, 7, 8, 9, 11, 13, 14, 15, 18, 19, 20, 21, 23, 24, 25, 26, 27, 28, 29, 31, 32, 35, 36, 37, 38,

39, 41, 43, 44, 46, 47, 50, 53, 54, 55,
56, 57, 58, 61, 64, 65, 66, 67, 68, 79,
98, 100, 106, 107, 110
fundraising, vii, 4, 7, 9, 30, 33, 36, 37,
44, 46, 57, 58, 66, 98
funds, vii, viii, 1, 3, 4, 5, 6, 7, 8, 11, 12,
13, 14, 15, 16, 17, 18, 19, 20, 21, 22,
23, 24, 25, 26, 27, 28, 29, 30, 31, 32,
33, 34, 35, 36, 37, 38, 39, 40, 41, 44,
45, 46, 47, 48, 49, 50, 51, 52, 53, 54,
56, 58, 61, 64, 65, 66, 67, 72, 74, 76,
78, 79, 80, 81, 85, 87, 88, 90, 92, 94,
98, 103, 111, 112

G

Gallup poll, 63, 64
gas, 15
gene, 71
general election, 3, 11, 12, 17, 18, 19,
20, 21, 22, 23, 25, 29, 32, 34, 35, 36,
41, 50, 53, 60, 65, 66, 71, 73, 74, 75,
76, 77, 78, 79, 80, 81, 82, 83, 84, 87,
88, 89, 90, 92, 93, 94, 95, 104
goals, 1, 7, 8, 57, 60
Gore, Al, 99
government, viii, 5, 8, 9, 12, 14, 15, 17,
20, 33, 37, 38, 64, 66, 105
government intervention, 9
GPO, 99, 100, 101, 102, 103, 104
grants, 7, 41
grassroots, 37
groups, vii, 3, 4, 7, 23, 30, 39, 61, 66, 97,
102, 105, 107
guidelines, 17

H

Hawaii, 43, 46, 49, 54, 58
hearing, 33
house, v, viii, 11, 15, 16, 17, 18, 19, 20,
21, 22, 23, 24, 25, 26, 27, 28, 29, 30,
31, 32, 33, 34, 38, 40, 46, 69, 70, 72,
74, 76, 78, 79, 80, 81, 82, 83, 84, 85,
87, 88, 89, 90, 91, 92, 95, 100, 101,
102, 103, 104
House Administration Committee, 20,
21, 22, 26, 27
household, 29, 32, 82, 83, 90
household income, 29, 32, 82, 83, 90

I

images, 41
implementation, 18, 26, 27, 38
incentives, 12, 17, 23, 31, 37, 40, 58, 66
inclusion, 35
income(s), 27, 29, 32, 40, 41, 55, 77, 82,
83, 90, 102, 105
income tax, 55, 105
increased competition, 60, 61
incumbents, 6, 8, 20, 34, 58, 60, 61, 108
independence, 15
indexing, 79, 92, 94
industry, 38
inequality, 15
infancy, 57
inferences, 68
inflation, 79
Information System, 104
inhibitor, 40
integrity, 4, 15
interest groups, vii, 4, 7, 23, 61, 66, 105,
107
intervention, 9
interviews, 60
issue advocacy, 3, 28, 66

J

Johnson, President Lyndon B., 17
judges, 56
judgment, 13
jurisdiction, 36

K

Kennedy, John F., 16
killing, 19

L

language, 30, 32, 97
law(s), 13, 16, 17, 18, 21, 39, 54, 56, 57,
 64, 67, 80, 97, 106, 111
leadership, 19, 21, 22, 25, 27, 34, 59, 61,
 68, 92, 94, 103
legislation, vii, 7, 18, 27, 28, 32, 41, 54,
 55, 56, 66, 68, 84, 91, 100, 101, 104
legislative elections, 57, 60, 65, 67, 68,
 107
legislative proposals, 5, 11
LexisNexis, 56
licenses, 38
licensing fees, 41
likelihood, 35
limitation, 55
linkage, 1, 2, 5
loans, 35, 71, 73, 75, 77, 102
lobbying, 27
lobbyists, 41, 80, 103
long-term impact, 61
Los Angeles, 106

M

machinery, 12, 13
Maine, 43, 45, 49, 53, 54, 58, 59, 60, 61,
 65, 110, 111
mainstream, 9
mandatory spending limits, vii, 5, 11, 29
market(s), 14, 31, 37, 38, 68, 92, 94
Maryland, 43, 46, 47, 49, 54, 107
Massachusetts, 43, 46, 50, 54, 98, 111
matching funds, vii, 3, 7, 11, 16, 19, 21,
 22, 26, 36, 40, 44, 46, 47, 65, 67
McCain, Senator John, 28

measures, 2, 7, 21, 34, 35, 36, 39, 57,
 107
media, 4, 8, 29, 30, 31, 37, 38, 55, 68,
 79, 88, 92, 94, 106
median, 29, 32, 82, 83, 90
men, 13, 14, 15
messages, 3, 9
Mexico, 43, 45, 51, 56
Minnesota, 43, 46, 50, 55, 58, 107, 108
minority(ies), 16, 59
models, 46, 59, 65, 66, 111
momentum, 20, 22, 28
money, vii, 3, 4, 5, 6, 7, 8, 9, 13, 16, 18,
 23, 26, 28, 29, 30, 31, 32, 33, 34, 35,
 36, 37, 39, 40, 44, 45, 46, 47, 53, 56,
 57, 58, 59, 60, 61, 63, 64, 65, 66, 67,
 68, 80, 81, 84, 87, 88, 89, 91, 92, 93,
 94, 95, 97, 102, 103, 106
motivation, 15

N

nation, 2, 16, 18, 36, 65
national parties, 13, 74, 97
natural gas, 15
NBC News poll, 64
Nebraska, 43, 46, 47, 51, 55, 66, 107
New Jersey, 43, 45, 46, 51, 55, 106
New Mexico, 43, 45, 51, 56
New York, 64, 99
New York Times, 64
North Carolina, 43, 45, 52, 56, 99

O

observations, 2
Ohio, 98
oil, 15
opinion polls, 4
organization(s), 4, 12, 13, 39, 45, 61, 68,
 97, 105, 107

P

PACs, 23, 28, 59, 61, 68, 80, 92, 94, 101, 102, 109
payroll, 15
penalty(ies), 13, 30, 31, 39, 55, 89, 93, 95
Pennsylvania, 112
perceptions, 7, 41
personal, 7, 8, 20, 35, 58, 72, 74, 76, 78, 109
personal wealth, 8
philosophical, 8, 33
policymakers, 2, 5, 34
policymaking, 33, 81, 89
political, 1, 2, 3, 4, 6, 7, 8, 9, 11, 12, 13, 14, 16, 17, 18, 23, 31, 34, 37, 38, 39, 43, 58, 64, 67, 68, 83, 91, 93, 94, 95, 97, 106, 108, 109, 111
political action committee, 23, 97
political appointments, 14
political parties, 3, 12, 16, 17, 43, 68, 83, 91, 94, 106, 108, 111
politicians, 5, 9, 33, 61
politics, 8, 45, 63, 66, 67
polling, 63, 64, 98, 111
population, 24, 34, 71, 78
power, 17
prediction, 4
president, 64, 104
President Bush, 26
presidential campaigns, 14, 17, 85
presidential elections, vii, 2, 3, 4, 5, 16, 17, 18, 19, 67, 83, 84, 90, 91, 100, 105
presidential veto, 25
pressure, 7, 17
price index, 31, 92, 94, 112
prices, 15
primaries, 3, 11, 16, 19, 20, 21, 26, 35, 36, 65, 66, 67, 83, 91
primary data, 110
primary elections, 21, 33, 66, 104
procedures, 32, 104

profit, 45, 75, 76, 77
program, 3, 8, 31, 32, 33, 45, 47, 51, 53, 54, 55, 56, 57, 58, 59, 60, 61, 65, 66, 68, 88, 92, 95, 105, 106, 107, 111
promote, 83, 90
property, 53
public debt, 19
public education, 32
public finance, 2, 4, 6, 17, 18, 19, 21, 22, 29, 33, 34, 39, 40, 57
public financing, vii, viii, 1, 2, 4, 5, 6, 7, 8, 9, 11, 14, 15, 16, 17, 18, 19, 20, 21, 22, 23, 24, 26, 28, 30, 31, 32, 33, 34, 37, 38, 39, 43, 44, 45, 46, 47, 51, 52, 53, 54, 55, 56, 57, 58, 59, 60, 61, 63, 64, 65, 66, 67, 68, 80, 87, 88, 90, 91, 92, 94, 95, 98, 104, 105, 106, 107, 108, 111, 112
public funding, viii, 3, 4, 5, 6, 7, 8, 9, 11, 13, 15, 19, 20, 21, 23, 25, 26, 29, 31, 35, 36, 37, 38, 39, 46, 50, 53, 58, 61, 64, 65, 66, 67, 79, 98, 107, 110
public funds, viii, 1, 3, 4, 5, 6, 12, 13, 20, 23, 24, 25, 29, 30, 31, 32, 33, 34, 35, 36, 37, 38, 39, 40, 41, 45, 47, 58, 61, 64, 66, 67, 98
public interest, 38
public money, vii, 36, 47, 66
public opinion, 2, 6, 7, 63, 98
public resources, 4, 12
public service, 83, 90
public support, viii, 6, 9, 35

R

race, 6, 60, 83, 90
radical, 12, 13
radio, 25, 26, 72
random, 82
range, 33, 41, 71, 73, 75, 77
recognition, 6, 18, 34
reconcile, 26
redistribution, 47
reelection, 4, 60

reforms, 4, 12, 20
regulation(s), 28, 63, 67, 97
Republican(s), 18, 22, 23, 25, 26, 27, 28, 32, 61
researchers, 9, 60, 105
reserves, 66
residential, 3, 13, 14, 64, 97
resistance, viii, 6
resolution, 14
resources, 3, 4, 6, 8, 12, 20, 31, 59, 67
restructuring, 30
returns, 3, 9, 19, 25, 72
revenue, 12, 24, 27, 31, 38
Rhode Island, 43, 46, 52, 56
roll-call votes, 25
Roosevelt, Theodore, 5, 12, 15, 99
Rules Committee, 26
runoff, 34, 80, 85

57, 64, 66, 67, 68, 71, 73, 75, 77, 83, 90, 100, 104
state office, 2
statutes, vii
strategic, 35
structuring, 36
subsidy(ies), vii, 2, 3, 4, 6, 7, 11, 12, 15, 16, 17, 19, 21, 23, 24, 25, 26, 27, 29, 36, 44, 45, 46, 48, 49, 50, 51, 52, 53, 55, 65, 67, 69, 70, 71, 73, 74, 75, 76, 77, 78, 80, 81, 87, 88, 91, 92, 93, 94, 95, 105, 111
summaries, 29
summer, 56
superiority, 15
Supreme Court, vii, 1, 2, 5, 8, 32, 51, 52, 53, 56, 82, 83, 89, 91, 93, 96, 104
systems, vii, viii, 2, 8, 26, 36, 40, 46, 57, 66, 104

S

salary, 79
scandal, 11, 18, 19, 20
science, 6, 34
Secretary of State, 48, 50, 51, 52, 53, 56
seed, 30, 31, 47, 80, 81, 87, 88, 92, 93, 94, 95
Senate, v, viii, 11, 12, 13, 14, 17, 18, 19, 20, 21, 23, 24, 25, 26, 27, 28, 29, 30, 31, 33, 34, 38, 39, 40, 69, 70, 71, 73, 75, 77, 83, 90, 91, 92, 93, 94, 95, 99, 100, 101, 102, 103, 104
Senate Finance Committee, 17, 30
series, 21
shape, 67
soft money, 3, 4, 26, 28, 32, 39, 84, 91, 102, 103
special interests, 7, 63, 64
spectrum, 31, 33, 92, 95, 104
speech, 9
spending limits, vii, 3, 5, 6, 7, 8, 20, 23, 24, 25, 26, 27, 28, 32, 33, 34, 35, 36, 38, 39, 40, 45, 47, 48, 49, 51, 53, 55,

T

tax credit, 7, 16, 18, 25, 26, 30, 37, 56, 72, 88, 92
tax deduction, 37
tax exemptions, 105
tax incentive, 12, 17, 31
tax increase, 105
tax reform, 37
taxation, 63
taxes, 40, 56
taxpayers, vii, 3, 4, 8, 9, 18, 40, 41, 105
telephone, 53, 54, 55, 56, 107, 110
television, 32, 90
term limits, 61
testimony, 7, 33, 98
theory, 44, 57
threat, 7, 18, 47
threshold level, 80
threshold(s), 21, 31, 36, 47, 80, 88, 89, 92, 93, 95, 96, 108
time frame, 32
timing, 63
trading, 14

transparency, 16
Treasury, 12, 13, 17, 37, 41, 83, 85, 90
treasury funds, 12
trust, 9, 33, 54, 111
trust fund, 54
turnout, 9, 60

U

U.S. Treasury, 12, 17, 37, 41, 90
uniform, 18, 46
unions, 80
United States, 8, 14, 83, 93, 96, 99, 103
universe, 59

V

variables, 40
Vermont, 43, 45, 52, 56
vetoed, viii, 11, 25, 26, 27, 40
Vice President, 13, 99
voluntary spending limits, vii, 1, 11, 22,
    23, 24, 35
voter turnout, 9

voters, 7, 15, 33, 36, 45, 54, 58, 66, 79,
    111
voting, 12, 22, 26, 34, 71, 78
vouchers, 24, 25, 26, 27, 31, 37, 41, 71,
    73, 75, 78, 91, 94

W

Washington, 64, 98, 99, 100, 101, 102,
    103, 104, 107, 109, 111
Washington Post, 64, 99
Watergate, 1, 11, 18, 19, 20, 36, 46
watershed, 28
wealth, 8
welfare, 9
winning, 9, 31, 80, 88
winter, 99
Wisconsin, 43, 46, 53, 56, 58, 67, 107,
    108
women, 59
writing, 2, 29, 33

Y

yield, 63